HBR'S 10 MUST READS

On
Communication

HBR's 10 Must Reads series is the definitive collection of ideas and best practices for aspiring and experienced leaders alike. These books offer essential reading selected from the pages of *Harvard Business Review* on topics critical to the success of every manager.

Titles include:

On
Communication

HARVARD BUSINESS REVIEW PRESS
Boston, Massachusetts

No part of this publication may be reproduced, stored in or introduced into a
retrieval system, or transmitted, in any form, or by any means (electronic,
mechanical, photocopying, recording, or otherwise), without the prior
permission of the publisher. Requests for permission should be directed to
permissions@hbsp.harvard.edu, or mailed to Permissions, Harvard Business
School Publishing, 60 Harvard Way, Boston, Massachusetts 02163.

The web addresses referenced in this book were live and correct at the time of
the book's publication but may be subject to change.

Library of Congress Cataloging-in-Publication Data

HBR's 10 must reads on communication.
        p. cm.
    Includes index.
    ISBN 978-1-4221-8986-3 (alk. paper)
    1. Business communication.   2. Communication in management.
3. Interpersonal communication.   I. Harvard business review.   II. Title:
HBR's ten must reads on communication.   III. Title: Harvard business
review's 10 must reads on communication.

    HF5718.H34 2013
    658.4'5—dc23   2012037908

ISBN: 9781422189863
eISBN: 9781422191514

The paper used in this publication meets the requirements of the American
National Standard for Permanence of Paper for Publications and Documents in
Libraries and Archives z39.48-1992.

Contents

On
Communication

Change the Way You Persuade

by Gary A. Williams and Robert B. Miller

IT'S HAPPENED TO YOU BEFORE. You call a meeting to try to convince your boss and peers that your company needs to make an important move—for instance, funding a risky but promising venture. Your argument is impassioned, your logic unassailable, your data bulletproof. Two weeks later, though, you learn that your brilliant proposal has been tabled. What went wrong?

All too often, people make the mistake of focusing too much on the content of their argument and not enough on how they deliver that message. Indeed, far too many decisions go the wrong way because information is presented ineffectively. In our experience, people can vastly improve their chances of having their proposals succeed by determining who the chief decision maker is among the executives they are trying to persuade and then tailoring their arguments to that business leader's decision-making style.

Specifically, we have found that executives typically fall into one of five decision-making categories: *Charismatics* can be initially exuberant about a new idea or proposal but will yield a final decision based on a balanced set of information. *Thinkers* can exhibit contradictory points of view within a single meeting and need to cautiously work through all the options before coming to a decision. *Skeptics* remain highly suspicious of data that don't fit with their worldview and make decisions based on their gut feelings. *Followers* make decisions based on how other trusted executives, or they themselves, have made similar decisions in the past. And *controllers* focus on the pure facts and analytics of a decision because of their own fears and uncertainties.

The five styles span a wide range of behaviors and characteristics. Controllers, for instance, have a strong aversion to risk; charismatics tend to seek it out. Despite such differences, people frequently use a one-size-fits-all approach when trying to convince their bosses, peers, and staff. They argue their case to a thinker the same way they would to a skeptic. Instead, managers should tailor their presentations to the executives they are trying to persuade, using the right buzzwords to deliver the appropriate information in the most effective sequence and format. After all, Bill Gates does not make decisions in the same way that Larry Ellison does. And knowing that can make a huge difference.

Five Approaches

Executives make it to the senior level largely because they are effective decision makers. Learning mostly from experience, they build a set of criteria that guides them. Each decision is influenced by both reason and emotion, but the weight given to each of these elements during the decision-making process can vary widely depending on the person.

In a two-year project, we studied the decision-making styles of more than 1,600 executives across a wide range of industries. Our work focused on how those people made purchasing decisions, but we contend that the results have broader applicability to decision making in general. We interviewed participants about various facets of their decision-making processes. For instance, how strong was their desire to have others educate them about the issues involved in a particular decision? How willing were they to move beyond the status quo? How much risk were they comfortable with in making the decision? These characteristics and preferences are often set early in a businessperson's career and evolve based on experience. In other words, people have a natural tendency toward a certain style of decision making that gets reinforced through successes— or that changes after repeated failures.

Idea in Brief

You call a meeting to try to convince your boss that your company needs to make an important move. Your argument is impassioned, your logic unassailable, your data bulletproof. Two weeks later, though, you learn that your brilliant proposal has been tabled. What went wrong? It's likely the proposal wasn't appropriately geared toward your boss's decision-making style, say consultants Gary Williams and Robert Miller. Over the course of several years' research, the authors have found that executives have a default style of decision making developed early in their careers. That style is reinforced through repeated successes or changed after several failures. Typically, the authors say, executives fall into one of five categories of decision-making styles: Charismatics are intrigued by new ideas, but experience has taught them to make decisions based on balanced information, not just on emotions. Thinkers are risk-averse and need as much data as possible before coming to decisions. Skeptics are suspicious of data that don't fit their worldview and, thus, make decisions based on their gut feelings. Followers make decisions based on how other trusted executives, or they themselves, have made similar decisions in the past. And controllers focus on the facts and analytics of decisions because of their own fears and uncertainties. But most business presentations aren't designed to acknowledge these different styles—to their detriment. In this article, the authors describe the various subtleties of the five decision-making styles and how best to persuade executives from each group. Knowing executives' preferences for hearing or seeing certain types of information at specific stages in their decision-making process can substantially improve your ability to tip the outcome in your favor, the authors conclude.

Our research should not be confused with standard personality tests and indicators like Myers-Briggs. Our framework is simply a categorization of how people tend to make decisions. Of course, people do not always make decisions in the same way; much depends on the situation they're in. But our research has shown that when it comes to making tough, high-stakes choices that involve many complex considerations and serious consequences, people tend to resort to a single, dominant style. Call it a default mode of decision making.

The Idea in Practice

Five Decision-Making Styles

Consider this fictional scenario: Sales and Marketing VP Mary Flood knows her company must become more customer focused. She recommends decentralizing her operations into regional account teams—but needs her CEO's support. Here's how she'd argue her case, *depending* on her CEO's decision-making style.

Style	Decision-Maker's Characteristics	Persuader's Strategy	Examples
CHARISMATIC Lee Iacocca, Herb Kelleher	Easily enthralled, but bases final decisions on balanced information Emphasizes bottom-line results	Focus on results. Make straight-forward arguments. Stress proposal's benefits with visual aids. Use buzzwords: **proven, actions, easy, clear.**	Diagrams current organization and problems, proposed restructuring and benefits—especially improved competitiveness. Explains potential challenges (resistance to staff relocation) and risk of inaction (losing largest customers). Provides detailed reports for CEO to review post-presentation.
THINKER Michael Dell, Bill Gates	Toughest to persuade Cerebral, logical Risk-averse Needs extensive detail	Present market research, customer surveys, case studies, cost/benefit analyses. Use buzzwords: **quality, numbers, expert, proof.**	Presents three different options in detail in first meeting. Explains data-gathering methods. Presents case studies of similar restructurings. Uses second meeting to fill argument gaps and recommend optimum plan. Waits weeks, months for CEO's decision.

In this article, we describe each of the five decision-making styles in detail. This information is intended to be neither exhaustive nor definitive, and most executives will exhibit only some of the traits we list. Nevertheless, knowing the general characteristics of the different styles can help you better tailor your presentations and arguments to your audience. Unfortunately, many people fail in this regard. In our experience, more than half of all sales presentations are mismatched to the decision maker's style. Specifically, close to

SKEPTIC Larry Ellison, Tom Siebel	Challenges every data point Decides based on gut feelings	Establish credibility with endorsements from someone the CEO trusts. Use buzzwords: **grasp, power, suspect, trust.**	Co-presents with trusted COO. Emphasizes information sources' credibility. Strokes CEO's ego ("You've probably seen this case study . . . "). Grounds arguments in real world.
FOLLOWER Peter Coors, Carly Fiorina	Relies on own or others' past decisions to make current choices Late adopter	Use testimonials to prove low risk. Present innovative, yet proven, solutions. Use buzzwords: **expertise, similar to, innovate, previous.**	Highlights case studies from other industries, but notes, "We could be the first in our industry to do this." Omits failed restructurings (though retains information in case CEO requests it). Presents three restructuring options. Uses multiple references to steer CEO toward her preferred choice; emphasizes option's affordability.
CONTROLLER Ross Perot, Martha Stewart	Unemotional, analytical Abhors uncertainty Only implements own ideas	Present highly structured arguments. Make listener "own" the idea. Avoid aggressive advocacy. Use buzzwords: **facts, reason, power, just do it.**	Over several months, continually sends CEO customer reports, marketing studies, financial projections. Emphasizes data highlighting company's problems. Identifies data contradictions, letting CEO analyze them. Waits for CEO to request meeting after large customer defects.

80% of all sales presentations focus on skeptics and controllers, but those two groups accounted for just 28% of the executives we surveyed.

To investigate the various subtleties of the five decision-making styles, we present the following hypothetical situation. In each of the subsequent sections devoted to explaining the categories, we will use this tale to demonstrate how our fictional protagonist should best argue her case to her CEO.

Five Styles of Decision Making—and the Ways to Influence Each

IN OUR RESEARCH, WE FOUND that executives typically have a default style of decision making that lands them in one of five distinct categories: charismatics, thinkers, skeptics, followers, and controllers.

From January 1999 to June 2001, we and our colleagues at Miller-Williams surveyed 1,684 executives to study their decision-making processes. The participants were from a range of industries (including automotive, retail, and high tech) and were interviewed by e-mail, in person, or over the telephone. The participants described their decision-making tendencies for our researchers—for instance, how long it took them to make a decision; their willingness to make a choice that might have negative consequences; their desire for others to educate them about the issues involved; and so on.

We performed a cluster analysis of these data and found that the executives' behaviors fell into the five groupings described below. The accuracy of the survey results reported in this article—for example, that 25% of the executives we interviewed were charismatics—is plus or minus 2.9%. For many of the prominent CEO examples cited, the categorizations are based on our firsthand observations and experiences with those executives; other categorizations are based on secondary sources, including media accounts.

	Charismatics	Thinkers	Skeptics	Followers	Controllers
Description	Charismatics account for 25% of all the executives we polled. They are easily intrigued and enthralled by new ideas, but experience has taught them to make final decisions based on balanced information, not just emotions.	Thinkers account for 11% of the executives we surveyed and can be the toughest executives to persuade. They are impressed with arguments that are supported by data. They tend to have a strong aversion to risk and can be slow to make a decision.	Skeptics account for 19% of the executives we polled. They tend to be highly suspicious of every data point presented, especially any information that challenges their worldview. They often have an aggressive, almost combative style and are usually described as take-charge people.	Followers account for 36% of all the executives we surveyed. They make decisions based on how they've made similar choices in the past or on how other trusted executives have made them. They tend to be risk-averse.	Controllers account for 9% of the executives we interviewed. They abhor uncertainty and ambiguity, and they will focus on the pure facts and analytics of an argument.

	Charismatics	Thinkers	Skeptics	Followers	Controllers
Typical Characteristics	enthusiastic, captivating, talkative, dominant	cerebral, intelligent, logical, academic	demanding, disruptive, disagreeable, rebellious	responsible, cautious, brand-driven, bargain-conscious	logical, unemotional, sensible, detail-oriented, accurate, analytical
Prominent Examples	Richard Branson, Lee Iacocca, Herb Kelleher	Michael Dell, Bill Gates, Katharine Graham	Steve Case, Larry Ellison, Tom Siebel	Peter Coors, Douglas Daft, Carly Fiorina	Jacques Nasser, Ross Perot, Martha Stewart
Buzzwords to Use	results, proven, actions, show, watch, easy, clear, focus	quality, academic, think, numbers, intelligent, plan, expert, proof	feel, grasp, power, action, suspect, trust, demand, disrupt	innovate, expedite, expertise, similar to, previous	details, facts, reason, logic, power, handle, physical, grab, just do it
Bottom Line	When trying to persuade a charismatic, fight the urge to join in his excitement. Focus the discussion on results. Make simple and straightforward arguments, and use visual aids to stress the features and benefits of your proposal.	Have lots of data ready. Thinkers need as much information as possible, including all pertinent market research, customer surveys, case studies, cost-benefit analyses, and so on. They want to understand all perspectives of a given situation.	You need as much credibility as you can garner. If you haven't established enough clout with a skeptic, you need to find a way to have it transferred to you prior to or during the meeting—for example, by gaining an endorsement from someone the skeptic trusts.	Followers tend to focus on proven methods; references and testimonials are big persuading factors. They need to feel certain that they are making the right decision—specifically, that others have succeeded in similar initiatives.	Your argument needs to be structured and credible. The controller wants details, but only if presented by an expert. Don't be too aggressive in pushing your proposal. Often, your best bet is to simply give him the information he needs and hope that he will convince himself.

MaxPro is a leading manufacturer of office equipment, including printers, photocopiers, and fax machines. The company has a centralized structure, with the bulk of its marketing and sales operations located at corporate headquarters. Mary Flood, the executive vice president of sales and marketing, knows she must restructure her operations to become more customer focused. Specifically, she needs to form major-account teams at the regional level instead of at the corporate level. All national accounts and targeted marketing would be based in one of five regions (Northeast, Southeast, Midwest, Southwest, and West), each run by a different vice president. In Flood's plan, account executives for MaxPro's major customers (clients with revenues over $50 million) would relocate near the headquarters of those companies and would report directly to their respective regional VP. Each region would have its own marketing team and distribution channels, leaving corporate marketing responsible just for brand development. Flood needs to persuade George Nolan, MaxPro's CEO, to approve these changes.

1. Charismatics

Charismatics (25% of all the executives we interviewed) are easily enthralled by new ideas. They can absorb large amounts of information rapidly, and they tend to process the world visually.

They want to move quickly from the big idea to the specifics—especially those details regarding implementation. Charismatics are often described as enthusiastic, captivating, talkative, dominant, and persistent. They are risk-seeking yet responsible individuals. They are impressed with intelligence and facts and not usually given to self-absorption and compulsiveness. Prominent examples of charismatics include Richard Branson, Lee Iacocca, Herb Kelleher, and Oprah Winfrey. (Note that many of the categorizations of the executives we cite in this article are based on our firsthand observations and experiences with them. Some are based on secondary sources, including media accounts.)

Although charismatics may show great exuberance for a new idea, getting a final commitment from them can be difficult. They've learned from experience—particularly from the bad decisions they've made—to temper their initial enthusiasm with a good dose of reality. They seek out facts to support their emotions, and if such data can't be found, they will quickly lose their enthusiasm for an idea. Furthermore, charismatics prefer arguments that are tied directly to bottom-line results and are particularly keen on proposals that will make their company more competitive. They are rarely convinced by one-sided arguments that lack a strong orientation toward results. At the end of the day, charismatics make their final decisions very methodically, and the decisions are based on balanced information.

When trying to persuade a charismatic, you need to fight the urge to join in his excitement. One approach is to slightly undersell the parts of your proposal that pique his interest. In other words, you should be prepared to merely acknowledge the items that he greets with enthusiasm and discuss the risks of each of those things. This will ground your proposal in reality and strengthen his confidence and trust in you. You also need to keep the discussion focused on results. Your arguments must be simple and straightforward, and you should use visual aids to stress the features and benefits of your proposal. If you don't provide this results-oriented information (even when it's not asked for), you risk that the charismatic will not have it later when he needs it. Furthermore, you should be very honest and up-front about the risks involved with accepting your proposal, while also delineating the measures that can help minimize those risks. If you try to conceal any potential downsides, you can be sure that the charismatic will discover them later—when you're not available to address any concerns he may have.

All executives are busy people, but the attention span of a charismatic can be particularly short. In a meeting, you need to start with the most critical information. Otherwise, you risk losing his attention if you take your time leading up to a crucial point. Even if you have a two-hour meeting scheduled, you might not get through your entire presentation. Charismatics disdain canned arguments and will often interrupt you to get to the bottom line. Indeed, charismatics prefer highly interactive meetings; at times, they will want to move around the room and take control of the discussion.

Although charismatics might appear to be independent thinkers, they often rely on other high-profile executives in the company when making major decisions. Addressing this tendency will help increase your chances of success. Also critical will be your quiet perseverance: Charismatics expect you to wait patiently for them to make a decision, which could take some time, even though their initial enthusiasm may have led you to believe otherwise. Buzzwords that can help hold a charismatic's interest include: results, proven, actions, show, watch, look, bright, easy, clear, and focus.

Persuasion in practice: Nolan the charismatic

Flood has scheduled an hour-long meeting with Nolan and the other members of the senior executive committee to discuss her proposed reorganization. Before that day, she previews her recommendations with COO Jack Warniers, Nolan's most trusted lieutenant. Warniers has several concerns about the restructuring, which Flood addresses and resolves through follow-up memos and e-mails.

Flood has prepared a few charts for the meeting, but these are merely for her own reference. Because she wants Nolan to feel like he can steer the discussion any which way, she will modify the charts in her head as necessary and redraw the information on a white board. Flood also knows that Nolan will at some point need all the details of the implementation—most of this information won't be discussed in the meeting—so she prepares a full report that she will give him afterward.

Flood starts her presentation by drawing a diagram that shows the current organization and its problems. Then she immediately jumps into her recommendations with a chart that outlines the new structure and how it will solve those problems.

She emphasizes how the reorganization will increase MaxPro's overall competitiveness. "The restructuring," she says, "will help us to better focus on our customers, and the result will be fewer defections, particularly among our important accounts." She delineates how the reorganization will help propel MaxPro ahead of the competition.

Flood's ideas initially appeal to Nolan, who likes bold, out-of-the-box solutions, and he starts talking about the new restructuring as if it's already been accomplished. To keep him grounded, Flood outlines the potential impact of the new structure. Specifically, she notes the cost of relocating staff and the strong possibility that the change will meet fierce resistance from several groups, including the IT division, which would be responsible for supporting a large number of employees in remote locations.

Next, Flood presents a detailed risk assessment of the implementation—what will happen if the reorganization fails and the steps the company can take to minimize those risks. This information is as much for Nolan as it is for the others in the company who will be charged with implementing the plan. She then talks about the risk of doing nothing by highlighting evidence that at least three of MaxPro's major customers are already considering switching to a competitor because they are dissatisfied with MaxPro's customer service.

Knowing that the charismatic Nolan will want to move forward quickly, Flood ends her presentation by asking what their next steps should be. Nolan requests a detailed schedule, with milestone dates, of how the reorganization might progress. "I thought you might be interested in that information," she says, "so I've included it in this report, along with supporting data from the research we've conducted so far, case studies of similar reorganizations at other companies, and other pertinent facts. In particular, you might want to look at the section on risk assessment." Flood also tells Nolan that there are two versions of the report: an executive summary and an in-depth analysis. That night, on a red-eye flight to the East Coast, Nolan starts thinking about Flood's proposal and begins wondering how the restructuring will affect MaxPro's biggest customers. He turns to her report and finds that information in the table "Impact on Our Ten Largest Customers."

2. Thinkers

Thinkers (11% of the executives we interviewed) are the most diffi-cult decision makers to understand and consequently the toughest to persuade.

They are often described as cerebral, intelligent, logical, and aca-demic. Typically, they are voracious readers and selective about the words they use. They are impressed with arguments that are quanti-tative and supported by data. Not usually known for their social skills, thinkers tend to guard their emotions. They have two strong visceral desires in business—to anticipate change and to win—and they often pride themselves on their ability to outthink and outma-neuver the competition. They are driven more by the need to retain control than by the need to innovate. Prominent examples include Michael Dell, Bill Gates, Katharine Graham, and Alan Greenspan.

Thinkers have a strong desire for comparative data, which can make it difficult to persuade them. To make a decision, they need as much information as possible, including all pertinent market research, customer surveys, case studies, cost-benefit analyses, and so on. Perhaps the single-most important piece of information thinkers need is the presenter's methodology for getting from point A to point B. They strive to understand all perspectives of a given situation. And, unlike charismatics, thinkers have a strong aversion to risk.

When trying to persuade thinkers, your best approach is to openly communicate your worries and concerns about your proposal, because thinkers work best when they know the risks up front. Often they will ask a battery of questions to explore and understand all the risks asso-ciated with an option. Thinkers can be swayed when the arguments and presentation appeal directly to their intelligence. Interestingly, their thought process is very selective but not always completely methodical. They will, for instance, sometimes circumvent their own decision-making processes if they feel a bargain—a relatively low-risk opportunity to save time or money—is in their best interest.

Thinkers will never forget a bad experience, so you need to make sure that your recommendations to them are truly the best options. (Of course, you should do this for any of the five types of decision makers, but particularly so with thinkers.) And anyway, thinkers will eventually figure out for themselves whether something was truly the best alternative, so you might be better off refraining from drawing conclusions for them. Otherwise you'll risk being seen as too helpful and potentially not credible. One effective strategy for persuading thinkers is to give them ample time and space to come to their own conclusions.

In a meeting, thinkers will often take contradictory points of view. This can be extremely confusing, but remember that thinkers do not like to show their cards up front, so expect that you may not be able to discern how they feel about any of the options you present. In fact, thinkers often do not reveal their intentions until they render their final decisions. Furthermore, they can be self-absorbed, so be prepared for silence as they digest the information you've given them. Buzzwords and phrases that will capture a thinker's attention include: quality, academic, think, numbers, makes sense, intelligent, plan, expert, competition, and proof.

Persuasion in practice: Nolan the thinker

To convince Nolan, Flood knows she must present as many data, facts, and figures as possible, so her strategy is to deliver that information in huge chunks over a long-enough period of time for him to absorb and make sense of everything. Consequently, she decides that her best approach is to present her argument over the course of two meetings.

In the first, she begins by making her best case for why MaxPro needs to restructure. She emphasizes that if things stay the same,

MaxPro will likely lose customers to competitors. (Interestingly, this piece of information—the risk of doing nothing—would be one of the last things she would present to Nolan if he were a charismatic. In fact, the order of presentation to a thinker is almost exactly the reverse order of presentation to a charismatic.)

Flood then explains how she arrived at the three options she has proposed for the restructuring. She details the methodology she used to gather and assess the data, and Nolan is quick to point out where she may have missed certain steps or made incorrect assumptions. This will benefit Flood in the long run, because Nolan is now taking ownership of her methodology.

Next, Flood highlights the pros and cons of each option, and she presents case studies of similar restructurings, including those from other industries and from different time periods. The case studies represent roughly an equal number of successes and failures. Flood points out why each was successful or why each failed, and from that she begins to write on a white board a list of reorganizing dos and don'ts, to which Nolan is quick to add his input.

Throughout her presentation, Flood is undaunted by Nolan's barrage of questions. She knows it's not a personal attack; it's an attack on her process or data. Flood is very up-front about where her data might be inconclusive or conflicting, where she's made assumptions using just her intuition, and areas where her argument is weak. Together, she and Nolan pick through the presentation. For one risk assessment that Flood has weighted as 60-40, for example, Nolan says it should be 50–50.

At the end of the first meeting, Flood draws up a to-do list that indicates where she needs to plug in more data or fill in gaps in her argument before the next meeting; Nolan helps her prioritize the list. In several instances, however, he says, "Well, I don't think we can get good data here, so let's just go by gut feel."

During the second meeting, Flood briefly summarizes what they discussed previously—with all the corrections and adjustments that Nolan has requested. Knowing that he hates surprises, she clearly points out anything new and different from the first presentation—for example, revised data. Next, using the updated information, she explains how she arrived at the optimum restructuring that maximizes the probability of success while keeping risks to an acceptable level. In conclusion, she shows the projected financial costs and additional revenues that the change will likely generate. After the meeting, Flood is prepared to wait weeks, if not months, for Nolan's decision.

3. Skeptics

Skeptics (19% of the executives we polled) are highly suspicious of every single data point, especially any information that challenges their worldview.

Perhaps the most defining trait of skeptics is that they tend to have very strong personalities. They can be demanding, disruptive, disagreeable, rebellious, and even antisocial. They may have an aggressive, almost combative style and are usually described as take-charge people. They tend to be self-absorbed and act primarily on their feelings. Prominent examples include Steve Case, Larry Ellison, and Tom Siebel.

During your presentation, a skeptic may get up and leave temporarily, take a phone call, or even carry on a side conversation for an extended period of time. He will be demanding of both your time and energy, locking horns with you whenever the opportunity arises. The thinker launches a volley of questions, and it is not personal; with a skeptic, it is. Do not let it get to you; just go through your presentation coolly and logically. The good news is that you will know almost immediately where you stand with skeptics. You can almost always depend on them to tell you what they are thinking because of their strong personalities.

To persuade a skeptic, you need as much credibility as you can garner. Skeptics tend to trust people who are similar to them—for instance, people who went to the same college or worked for the same companies. If you haven't established credibility with a skeptic, you need to find a way to have it transferred to you prior to or during the meeting—for example, by gaining an endorsement from someone the skeptic trusts. Doing this will let the skeptic maintain his superior position while allowing you to openly discuss issues on his level. Credibility can be transferred (from a colleague, for instance), but ultimately it must be earned, and you may have to go through some very aggressive questioning to establish it.

Challenging a skeptic is risky and must be handled delicately. Sometimes, to make your case, you will need to correct bad information that the skeptic is relying on. If, for instance, the skeptic states incorrectly that your company's R&D costs have been spiraling out of control recently, you might reply, "Are you testing me? Because I remember you telling me a couple months ago that we need to spend more to regain our leadership in developing innovative products. But maybe that's changed?" In other words, when you need to correct a skeptic, give him room to save face. For him to trust you, he needs to maintain his reputation and ego. And remember that skeptics do not like being helped; they prefer having people think they know something already.

Although persuading a skeptic might sound daunting, the process is actually very straightforward. Skeptics want to move forward with groundbreaking ideas, but they first need to make sure that those ideas are from people they fully trust. Skeptics usually make decisions quickly—within days, if not right on the spot. Buzzwords to use with a skeptic include: feel, grasp, power, action, suspect, trust, agreeable, demand, and disrupt.

Persuasion in practice: Nolan the skeptic

Flood knows that she lacks the necessary clout to make her pitch directly to Nolan. So she enlists the aid of COO Jack Warniers, whom Nolan trusts. After she obtains Warniers's buy-in, she asks him to copresent the idea with her, hoping that his credibility will add to hers. They agree beforehand that Warniers will deliver all key messages, including the proposed restructuring and any data that might be controversial.

At the meeting, Flood and Warniers make their arguments in roughly the same order they would if Nolan were a thinker instead of a skeptic, but they emphasize the credibility of all their information sources. Flood knows that Nolan needs to hear things from multiple reputable sources—the more the better. So when discussing a recent marketing survey, she says, "I took the liberty of arranging a call between you and several other local market-research experts to discuss these results in greater detail." Whenever Nolan challenges anything, Flood and Warniers work quickly to ease his discomfort. Knowing that Nolan respects Bill Gates, for example, Flood softens one of Nolan's attacks by saying, "I see your point, but you probably remember that Microsoft made a similar move about two years ago."

At every turn, Flood and Warniers are careful to tread lightly around Nolan's ego. When discussing the case studies, for instance, they introduce each one by saying, "You've probably seen this before . . ." or "As you know, Hewlett-Packard failed in a similar restructuring because. . . ." For each example, Flood and Warniers are quick to point out whether the company's image and reputation were enhanced or degraded as a result of the restructuring.

Because Nolan is particularly skeptical of anything abstract, Flood and Warniers are careful to make their arguments as concrete as possible, usually by grounding them in the real world. When they talk about relocating 200 employees, for example, they try to include the specifics: "We would need to close our building here on Hunter Avenue and sublease the space, including the adjacent parking lot. Because the building has a modular, funky layout, we might consider turning it into a business incubator."

At the end of their presentation, Flood and Warniers appeal to Nolan's rebellious streak by stating how the proposed reorganization would buck the trend in their industry. They also are quick to credit Nolan for inspiring the idea. "At the last meeting of the senior executive committee," Warniers says, "you talked about how we needed to ensure that we didn't lose touch with our customers. Your comment started us thinking about this restructuring." Flood and Warniers end their presentation with their proposed action plan for the reorganization, complete with a schedule of milestones. At that point, Nolan takes charge of the discussion.

4. Followers

Followers (36% of the executives we interviewed) make decisions based on how they've made similar choices in the past or on how other trusted executives have made them.

Because they are afraid of making the wrong choice, followers will seldom be early adopters. Instead, they trust in known brands and in bargains, both of which represent less risk. They are also very good at seeing the world through other people's eyes. Interestingly, despite their cautiousness, followers can be spontaneous at times. Above all, though, they are responsible decision makers, which is why they are most often found in large corporations. In fact, followers account for more than a third of all the executives we surveyed, representing the largest group among the five types of decision makers. Prominent examples include Peter Coors, Douglas Daft, and Carly Fiorina.

Followers may engage you in long lists of issues and repeatedly challenge your position (similar to what a skeptic does), but don't be fooled. In the end, they will agree to something only if they've seen it done elsewhere. But followers won't admit this. In fact, they will seldom concede that they are followers; they would much rather have you believe that they are innovative and forward thinking. Frequently, followers are mistaken for skeptics. However, followers are not inherently suspicious; they prefer that you help them gain a better grasp of what they don't understand. And although followers may exhibit a take-charge approach, they will yield when challenged. (As a general rule, people who are difficult to classify into a decision-making style are usually followers, because people in the other four groups tend to show their characteristics more definitively.)

Although followers are often the most difficult to identify, they can be the easiest to persuade—if you know which buttons to push. To obtain buy-in from a follower, you need to make him feel confident about deciding to move in a certain direction by proving that others have succeeded on that path. Not surprisingly, followers tend to focus on proven methods, and references and testimonials are big persuading factors.

With a follower, don't try to sell yourself unless you have a strong track record of success. Instead, look for past decisions by the follower that support your views or find similar decisions by other executives the follower trusts. Ideally, followers want solutions that are innovative yet proven, new but trusted, leading-edge yet somewhat safe. At the end of the day, though, what followers need most is to know that they won't lose their jobs. This is why they rarely make out-of-the-box decisions. In fact, for some followers, the only way to persuade them to adopt a truly bold strategy is to get someone else to do it successfully first. Buzzwords and phrases to use with a follower include: innovate, expedite, swift, bright, just like before, expertise, similar to, previous, what works, and old way.

Persuasion in practice: Nolan the follower

Flood knows that her mission is simple: She must make Nolan feel comfortable that the decision to restructure has minimal risk. And to seal the deal, she must somehow also make him feel that he is being innovative.

In the meeting, Flood presents her arguments in roughly the same order that she would if Nolan were a thinker or skeptic. But because Nolan is a follower, Flood emphasizes the case studies—eight of them in all. This discussion resonates with Nolan because, like all followers, he is particularly adept at placing himself in others' shoes. As part of her strategy, Flood has decided to omit any examples of failed restructurings—but she has that information on hand, just in case Nolan asks for it. The eight case studies are from industries outside of MaxPro's business so that Flood can appeal to Nolan's desire to be innovative by saying, "We could be the first in our industry to do this kind of restructuring."

Next, Flood presents three options for the proposed restructuring, and she links each of her case studies to one of those options. To steer Nolan toward option three, which she prefers, she has linked four of the cases to that option; by contrast, she has provided Nolan with only two case study references for each of the other two options. When Nolan notes that option one is the cheapest, Flood is ready to address that issue head-on because she knows how bargain conscious he is: Her detailed analysis shows that, on a risk-adjusted basis, option three is actually the least expensive because it is more proven.

Presenting three options to Nolan does more than just give him the opportunity to make a choice; it also affords him the chance to be creative. He begins to combine aspects of options one and three—something Flood had anticipated he would do. In fact, she has even encouraged him to do so by presenting certain minor components of the different options individually. For Nolan, the ability to mix and match different parts of proven strategies is perfect: It makes him feel innovative without having to incur any major risk.

At the conclusion of the meeting, Flood further plays on Nolan's desire for both innovation and security by saying, "Yes, other companies have done this type of restructuring, but we will have more expertise implementing it, so we will do it faster and more cheaply. And because we already know what works and what doesn't, we'll be able to take the appropriate steps to avoid potential problems."

Flood understands that followers will maintain the status quo unless they're presented with information they can't afford to ignore. Because Nolan seems genuinely engrossed in hearing how the other companies have successfully reorganized, Flood expects she will hear from him within days. (Followers tend to act quickly once they see big potential for success with minimal risk.)

5. Controllers

Controllers (9% of the executives we surveyed) abhor uncertainty and ambiguity, and they will focus on the pure facts and analytics of an argument. They are both constrained and driven by their own fears and insecurities.

They are usually described as logical, unemotional, sensible, detail oriented, accurate, analytical, and objective. Like skeptics, controllers often have strong personalities and can even be overbearing. In their minds, they are the best salespeople, the best marketing experts, the best strategists, and so on. Whereas followers are good at putting themselves in others' shoes, controllers see things only from their own perspectives and will frequently make snap judgments and remarks that alienate others. Controllers can be loners and are often self-absorbed, traits that lead them to make unilateral decisions. Indeed, although a controller may talk to others about a decision, he will seldom genuinely listen to them or consider their input. Prominent examples include Jacques Nasser, Ross Perot, and Martha Stewart.

When dealing with controllers, you need to overcome their internal fears, which they will pretend they don't have. In fact, they will cover them up by paying an inordinate amount of attention to the intricate details of processes and methods. Dealing with controllers can be like playing a game of cat and mouse—you will always be chasing down some information at their request.

In a meeting, remember that controllers can be self-absorbed, so be prepared for long silences during your interactions. It is also crucial to remember that when cornered, controllers rarely capitulate. Furthermore, even though controllers seek accuracy and facts, that does not necessarily mean they will make intelligent, rational decisions. Often, a controller will jump to illogical conclusions. And unlike charismatics, who are willing to take responsibility for their decisions, controllers try to avoid being held accountable. When something goes wrong, they assume others are at fault.

To persuade controllers, your argument needs to be structured, linear, and credible. They want details, but only if presented by an expert. In practice, the only way to sell an idea to controllers is not to sell it; instead, let them make the choice to buy. Your best bet is to simply supply them with the information they need and hope they will convince themselves.

Although controllers and skeptics share several characteristics, a key difference is that controllers need ample time to make decisions (they hate to be rushed). By contrast, skeptics are much quicker on the draw. One of the worst things you can do with a controller is to push your proposal too aggressively. When that happens, controllers are likely to see you as part of the problem and not the solution. Buzzwords and phrases to use with a controller include: details, facts, reason, logic, power, handle, physical, grab, keep them honest, make them pay, and just do it.

Persuasion in practice: Nolan the controller

Nolan is notorious for implementing only his own ideas, so Flood knows she must somehow make him take ownership of her proposed restructuring plan. To do that, she gears herself up for the long journey ahead. Over the course of several months, she continually sends him information—customer reports, marketing studies, financial projections, and so on—through all types of media (including print, video, and the Web) and in person. She needs to gently wear down his defenses by steadily supplying him with so much information that he simply has to make a decision.

First, Flood focuses on data that highlight MaxPro's problems because she knows that case studies and other information won't be as important to him. Her memos often prompt Nolan to request other information, sometimes arcane and irrelevant data. She gets this for him, knowing full well that he may not even look at it.

After four months she is tempted to schedule a formal presentation, but she resists the urge. Nolan himself must request that meeting. Until that time, she will have to be content with sending him still more information. When she does, she always provides the information in a structured, linear format. In a typical memo, she begins by writing, "Attached, please find the results from a recent customer survey, and here's how they fit in with the other material we have." Flood is also quick to point out (but not resolve) apparent contradictions in the data, knowing that Nolan prides himself in uncovering those kinds of inconsistencies. In one memo, she writes, "Here's some new research from Walker Consulting. It seems to contradict the study we commissioned last year. I'm not sure which to trust."

Finally, an event—the defection of one of MaxPro's largest customers—triggers action. Thanks to Flood's patient but incessant prodding, Nolan is sensitized to this latest development. He calls a meeting of the senior staff to discuss what MaxPro should do. Included will be a discussion of a possible reorganization.

Critics might view some of our categorizations as derogatory—after all, few executives would like being classified as followers or controllers. We do not intend to imply that any decision-making style is superior to another; our labels are merely brief descriptors of the primary behavior of each group. In fact, each style can be highly effective in certain environments. Followers, for instance, have a high sense of responsibility and can be excellent leaders at large, established corporations. And controllers can be extremely effective business leaders; Martha Stewart is a case in point.

Furthermore, we do not mean to oversimplify the complex and often mysterious ways in which people reach conclusions. To be sure, decision making is a complicated, multifaceted process that researchers may never fully unpick. That said, we strongly believe that executives tend to make important decisions in predictable ways. And knowing their preferences for hearing or seeing certain types of information at specific stages in their decision-making process can substantially improve your ability to tip the outcome your way.

Originally published in May 2002. Reprint R0205D

Harnessing the Science of Persuasion

by Robert B. Cialdini

A LUCKY FEW HAVE IT; most of us do not. A handful of gifted "naturals" simply know how to capture an audience, sway the undecided, and convert the opposition. Watching these masters of persuasion work their magic is at once impressive and frustrating. What's impressive is not just the easy way they use charisma and eloquence to convince others to do as they ask. It's also how eager those others are to do what's requested of them, as if the persuasion itself were a favor they couldn't wait to repay.

The frustrating part of the experience is that these born persuaders are often unable to account for their remarkable skill or pass it on to others. Their way with people is an art, and artists as a rule are far better at doing than at explaining. Most of them can't offer much help to those of us who possess no more than the ordinary quotient of charisma and eloquence but who still have to wrestle with leadership's fundamental challenge: getting things done through others. That challenge is painfully familiar to corporate executives, who every day have to figure out how to motivate and direct a highly individualistic work force. Playing the "Because I'm the boss" card is out. Even if it weren't demeaning and demoralizing for all concerned, it would be out of place in a world where cross-functional teams, joint ventures, and intercompany partnerships have blurred the lines of authority. In such an environment, persuasion skills exert far greater influence over others' behavior than formal power structures do.

Which brings us back to where we started. Persuasion skills may be more necessary than ever, but how can executives acquire them if the most talented practitioners can't pass them along? By looking to science. For the past five decades, behavioral scientists have conducted experiments that shed considerable light on the way certain interactions lead people to concede, comply, or change. This research shows that persuasion works by appealing to a limited set of deeply rooted human drives and needs, and it does so in predictable ways. Persuasion, in other words, is governed by basic principles that can be taught, learned, and applied. By mastering these principles, executives can bring scientific rigor to the business of securing consensus, cutting deals, and winning concessions. In the pages that follow, I describe six fundamental principles of persuasion and suggest a few ways that executives can apply them in their own organizations.

The Principle of Liking

People like those who like them.

The application
Uncover real similarities and offer genuine praise.

The retailing phenomenon known as the Tupperware party is a vivid illustration of this principle in action. The demonstration party for Tupperware products is hosted by an individual, almost always a woman, who invites to her home an array of friends, neighbors, and relatives. The guests' affection for their hostess predisposes them to buy from her, a dynamic that was confirmed by a 1990 study of purchase decisions made at demonstration parties. The researchers, Jonathan Frenzen and Harry Davis, writing in the *Journal of Consumer Research,* found that the guests' fondness for their hostess weighed twice as heavily in their purchase decisions as their regard for the products they bought. So when guests at a Tupperware party

Idea in Brief

If leadership, at its most basic, consists of getting things done through others, then persuasion is one of the leader's essential tools. Many executives have assumed that this tool is beyond their grasp, available only to the charismatic and the eloquent. Over the past several decades, though, experimental psychologists have learned which methods reliably lead people to concede, comply, or change. Their research shows that persuasion is governed by several principles that can be taught and applied. The first principle is that people are more likely to follow someone who is similar to them than someone who is not. Wise managers, then, enlist peers to help make their cases. Second, people are more willing to cooperate with those who are not only like them but who like them, as well. So it's worth the time to uncover real similarities and offer genuine praise. Third, experiments

confirm the intuitive truth that people tend to treat you the way you treat them. It's sound policy to do a favor before seeking one. Fourth, individuals are more likely to keep promises they make voluntarily and explicitly. The message for managers here is to get commitments in writing. Fifth, studies show that people really do defer to experts. So before they attempt to exert influence, executives should take pains to establish their own expertise and not assume that it's self-evident. Finally, people want more of a commodity when it's scarce; it follows, then, that exclusive information is more persuasive than widely available data. By mastering these principles—and, the author stresses, using them judiciously and ethically—executives can learn the elusive art of capturing an audience, swaying the undecided, and converting the opposition.

buy something, they aren't just buying to please themselves. They're buying to please their hostess as well.

What's true at Tupperware parties is true for business in general: If you want to influence people, win friends. How? Controlled research has identified several factors that reliably increase liking, but two stand out as especially compelling—similarity and praise. Similarity literally draws people together. In one experiment, reported in a 1968 article in the *Journal of Personality,* participants stood physically closer to one another after learning that they shared political beliefs and social values. And in a 1963 article in *American Behavioral Scientists,* researcher F. B. Evans used demographic data from insurance

The Idea in Practice

Persuasion Principles

Principle	Example	Business Application
LIKING: People like those like them, who like them.	At Tupperware parties, guests' fondness for their host influences purchase decisions twice as much as regard for the products.	**To influence people, win friends,** through: *Similarity*: Create *early* bonds with new peers, bosses, and direct reports by informally discovering common interests—you'll establish goodwill and trustworthiness. *Praise*: Charm *and* disarm. Make positive remarks about others—you'll generate more willing compliance.
RECIPROCITY: People repay in kind.	When the Disabled American Veterans enclosed free personalized address labels in donation-request envelops, response rate doubled.	**Give what you want to receive.** Lend a staff member to a colleague who needs help; you'll get *his* help later.
SOCIAL PROOF: People follow the lead of similar others.	More New York City residents tried returning a lost wallet after learning that other New Yorkers had tried.	**Use peer power** to influence horizontally, not vertically; e.g., ask an esteemed "old timer" to support your new initiative if other veterans resist.

company records to demonstrate that prospects were more willing to purchase a policy from a salesperson who was akin to them in age, religion, politics, or even cigarette-smoking habits.

Managers can use similarities to create bonds with a recent hire, the head of another department, or even a new boss. Informal conversations during the workday create an ideal opportunity to discover at least one common area of enjoyment, be it a hobby, a college basketball team, or reruns of *Seinfeld*. The important thing is to establish the bond early because it creates a presumption of goodwill and trustworthiness in every subsequent encounter. It's much easier

CONSISTENCY: People fulfill written, public, and voluntary commitments.	92% of residents of an apartment complex who signed a petition supporting a new recreation center later donated money to the cause.	**Make others' commitments active, public, and voluntary.** If you supervise an employee who should submit reports on time, get that understanding in writing (a memo); make the commitment public (note colleagues' agreement with the memo); and link the commitment to the employee's values (the impact of timely reports on team spirit).
AUTHORITY: People defer to experts who provide shortcuts to decisions requiring specialized information.	A single *New York Times* expert-opinion news story aired on TV generates a 4% shift in U.S. public opinion.	**Don't assume your expertise is self-evident.** Instead, establish your expertise *before* doing business with new colleagues or partners; e.g., in conversations before an important meeting, describe how you solved a problem similar to the one on the agenda.
SCARCITY: People value what's scarce.	Wholesale beef buyers' orders jumped 600% when they alone received information on a possible beef shortage.	**Use exclusive information to persuade.** Influence and rivet key players' attention by saying, for example: ". . . Just got this information today. It won't be distributed until next week."

to build support for a new project when the people you're trying to persuade are already inclined in your favor.

Praise, the other reliable generator of affection, both charms and disarms. Sometimes the praise doesn't even have to be merited. Researchers at the University of North Carolina writing in the *Journal of Experimental Social Psychology* found that men felt the greatest regard for an individual who flattered them unstintingly even if the comments were untrue. And in their book *Interpersonal Attraction* (Addison-Wesley, 1978), Ellen Berscheid and Elaine Hatfield Walster presented experimental data showing that positive remarks about another person's traits, attitude, or performance reliably generates liking in return, as well as willing compliance with the wishes of the person offering the praise.

Along with cultivating a fruitful relationship, adroit managers can also use praise to repair one that's damaged or unproductive. Imagine you're the manager of a good-sized unit within your organization. Your work frequently brings you into contact with another manager—call him Dan—whom you have come to dislike. No matter how much you do for him, it's not enough. Worse, he never seems to believe that you're doing the best you can for him. Resenting his attitude and his obvious lack of trust in your abilities and in your good faith, you don't spend as much time with him as you know you should; in consequence, the performance of both his unit and yours is deteriorating.

The research on praise points toward a strategy for fixing the relationship. It may be hard to find, but there has to be something about Dan you can sincerely admire, whether it's his concern for the people in his department, his devotion to his family, or simply his work ethic. In your next encounter with him, make an appreciative comment about that trait. Make it clear that in this case at least, you value what he values. I predict that Dan will relax his relentless negativity and give you an opening to convince him of your competence and good intentions.

The Principle of Reciprocity

People repay in kind.

The application
Give what you want to receive.

Praise is likely to have a warming and softening effect on Dan because, ornery as he is, he is still human and subject to the universal human tendency to treat people the way they treat him. If you have ever caught yourself smiling at a coworker just because he or she smiled first, you know how this principle works.

Charities rely on reciprocity to help them raise funds. For years, for instance, the Disabled American Veterans organization, using only a well-crafted fund-raising letter, garnered a very respectable 18% rate of response to its appeals. But when the group started enclosing a small gift in the envelope, the response rate nearly doubled to 35%. The gift—personalized address labels—was extremely modest, but it wasn't what prospective donors received that made the difference. It was that they had gotten anything at all.

What works in that letter works at the office, too. It's more than an effusion of seasonal spirit, of course, that impels suppliers to shower gifts on purchasing departments at holiday time. In 1996, purchasing managers admitted to an interviewer from *Inc.* magazine that after having accepted a gift from a supplier, they were willing to purchase products and services they would have otherwise declined. Gifts also have a startling effect on retention. I have encouraged readers of my book to send me examples of the principles of influence at work in their own lives. One reader, an employee of the State of Oregon, sent a letter in which she offered these reasons for her commitment to her supervisor:

> He gives me and my son gifts for Christmas and gives me presents on my birthday. There is no promotion for the type of job I have, and my only choice for one is to move to another department. But I find myself resisting trying to move. My boss is reaching retirement age, and I am thinking I will be able to move out after he retires. . . . [F]or now, I feel obligated to stay since he has been so nice to me.

Ultimately, though, gift giving is one of the cruder applications of the rule of reciprocity. In its more sophisticated uses, it confers a genuine first-mover advantage on any manager who is trying to foster positive attitudes and productive personal relationships in the office: Managers can elicit the desired behavior from coworkers and employees by displaying it first. Whether it's a sense of trust, a spirit of cooperation, or a pleasant demeanor, leaders should model the behavior they want to see from others.

The same holds true for managers faced with issues of information delivery and resource allocation. If you lend a member of your staff to a colleague who is shorthanded and staring at a fast-approaching deadline, you will significantly increase your chances of getting help when you need it. Your odds will improve even more if you say, when your colleague thanks you for the assistance, something like, "Sure, glad to help. I know how important it is for me to count on your help when I need it."

The Principle of Social Proof

People follow the lead of similar others.

The application
Use peer power whenever it's available.

Social creatures that they are, human beings rely heavily on the people around them for cues on how to think, feel, and act. We know this intuitively, but intuition has also been confirmed by experiments, such as the one first described in 1982 in the *Journal of Applied Psychology*. A group of researchers went door-to-door in Columbia, South Carolina, soliciting donations for a charity campaign and displaying a list of neighborhood residents who had already donated to the cause. The researchers found that the longer the donor list was, the more likely those solicited would be to donate as well.

To the people being solicited, the friends' and neighbors' names on the list were a form of social evidence about how they should respond. But the evidence would not have been nearly as compelling had the names been those of random strangers. In an experiment from the 1960s, first described in the *Journal of Personality and Social Psychology,* residents of New York City were asked to return a lost wallet to its owner. They were highly likely to attempt to return the wallet when they learned that another New Yorker had previously attempted to do so. But learning that someone from a foreign country had tried to return the wallet didn't sway their decision one way or the other.

The lesson for executives from these two experiments is that persuasion can be extremely effective when it comes from peers. The science supports what most sales professionals already know: Testimonials from satisfied customers work best when the satisfied customer and the prospective customer share similar circumstances. That lesson can help a manager faced with the task of selling a new corporate initiative. Imagine that you're trying to streamline your department's work processes. A group of veteran employees is resisting. Rather than try to convince the employees of the move's merits yourself, ask an old-timer who supports the initiative to speak up for it at a team meeting. The compatriot's testimony stands a much better chance of convincing the group than yet another speech from the boss. Stated simply, influence is often best exerted horizontally rather than vertically.

The Principle of Consistency

People align with their clear commitments.

The application
Make their commitments active, public, and voluntary.

Liking is a powerful force, but the work of persuasion involves more than simply making people feel warmly toward you, your idea, or your product. People need not only to like you but to feel committed to what you want them to do. Good turns are one reliable way to make people feel obligated to you. Another is to win a public commitment from them.

My own research has demonstrated that most people, once they take a stand or go on record in favor of a position, prefer to stick to it. Other studies reinforce that finding and go on to show how even a small, seemingly trivial commitment can have a powerful effect on future actions. Israeli researchers writing in 1983 in the *Personality and Social Psychology Bulletin* recounted how they asked half the residents of a large apartment complex to sign a petition favoring the establishment of a recreation center for the handicapped. The cause was good and the request was small, so almost everyone who was asked agreed to sign. Two weeks later, on National Collection Day for the Handicapped, all residents of the complex were approached at home and asked to give to the cause. A little more than half of those who were not asked to sign the petition made a contribution. But an astounding 92% of those who did sign donated money. The residents of the apartment complex felt obligated to live up to their commitments because those commitments were active, public, and voluntary. These three features are worth considering separately.

There's strong empirical evidence to show that a choice made actively—one that's spoken out loud or written down or otherwise made explicit—is considerably more likely to direct someone's future conduct than the same choice left unspoken. Writing in 1996 in the *Personality and Social Psychology Bulletin,* Delia Cioffi and Randy Garner described an experiment in which college students in one group were asked to fill out a printed form saying they wished to volunteer for an AIDS education project in the public schools. Students in another group volunteered for the same project by leaving blank a form stating that they didn't want to participate. A few days later, when the volunteers reported for duty, 74% of those who showed up were students from the group that signaled their commitment by filling out the form.

The implications are clear for a manager who wants to persuade a subordinate to follow some particular course of action: Get it in writing. Let's suppose you want your employee to submit reports in a more timely fashion. Once you believe you've won agreement, ask him to summarize the decision in a memo and send it to you. By doing so, you'll have greatly increased the odds that he'll fulfill the commitment because, as a rule, people live up to what they have written down.

Research into the social dimensions of commitment suggests that written statements become even more powerful when they're made public. In a classic experiment, described in 1955 in the *Journal of Abnormal and Social Psychology,* college students were asked to estimate the length of lines projected on a screen. Some students were asked to write down their choices on a piece of paper, sign it, and hand the paper to the experimenter. Others wrote their choices on an erasable slate, then erased the slate immediately. Still others were instructed to keep their decisions to themselves.

The experimenters then presented all three groups with evidence that their initial choices may have been wrong. Those who had merely kept their decisions in their heads were the most likely to reconsider their original estimates. More loyal to their first guesses were the students in the group that had written them down and immediately erased them. But by a wide margin, the ones most reluctant to shift from their original choices were those who had signed and handed them to the researcher.

This experiment highlights how much most people wish to appear consistent to others. Consider again the matter of the employee who has been submitting late reports. Recognizing the power of this desire, you should, once you've successfully convinced him of the need to be more timely, reinforce the commitment by making sure it gets a public airing. One way to do that would be to send the employee an e-mail that reads, "I think your plan is just what we need. I showed it to Diane in manufacturing and Phil in shipping, and they thought it was right on target, too." Whatever way such commitments are formalized, they should never be like the New Year's resolutions people privately make and then abandon with no one the wiser. They should be publicly made and visibly posted.

More than 300 years ago, Samuel Butler wrote a couplet that explains succinctly why commitments must be voluntary to be lasting and effective: "He that complies against his will/Is of his own opinion still." If an undertaking is forced, coerced, or imposed from the outside, it's not a commitment; it's an unwelcome burden. Think how you would react if your boss pressured you to donate to the campaign of a political candidate. Would that make you more apt to opt for that candidate in the privacy of a voting booth? Not likely. In fact, in their 1981 book *Psychological Reactance* (Academic Press), Sharon S. Brehm and Jack W. Brehm present data that suggest you'd vote the opposite way just to express your resentment of the boss's coercion.

This kind of backlash can occur in the office, too. Let's return again to that tardy employee. If you want to produce an enduring change in his behavior, you should avoid using threats or pressure tactics to gain

Persuasion Experts, Safe at Last

THANKS TO SEVERAL DECADES OF rigorous empirical research by behavioral scientists, our understanding of the how and why of persuasion has never been broader, deeper, or more detailed. But these scientists aren't the first students of the subject. The history of persuasion studies is an ancient and honorable one, and it has generated a long roster of heroes and martyrs.

A renowned student of social influence, William McGuire, contends in a chapter of the *Handbook of Social Psychology,* 3rd ed. (Oxford University Press, 1985) that scattered among the more than four millennia of recorded Western history are four centuries in which the study of persuasion flourished as a craft. The first was the Periclean Age of ancient Athens, the second occurred during the years of the Roman Republic, the next appeared in the time of the European Renaissance, and the last extended over the hundred years that have just ended, which witnessed the advent of large-scale advertising, information, and mass media campaigns. Each of the three previous centuries of systematic persuasion study was marked by a flowering of human achievement that was suddenly cut short when political authorities had the masters

his compliance. He'd likely view any change in his behavior as the result of intimidation rather than a personal commitment to change. A better approach would be to identify something that the employee genuinely values in the workplace—high-quality workmanship, perhaps, or team spirit—and then describe how timely reports are consistent with those values. That gives the employee reasons for improvement that he can own. And because he owns them, they'll continue to guide his behavior even when you're not watching.

The Principle of Authority

People defer to experts.

The application
Expose your expertise; don't assume it's self-evident.

Two thousand years ago, the Roman poet Virgil offered this simple counsel to those seeking to choose correctly: "Believe an expert." That may or may not be good advice, but as a description of what of persuasion killed. The philosopher Socrates is probably the best known of the persuasion experts to run afoul of the powers that be.

Information about the persuasion process is a threat because it creates a base of power entirely separate from the one controlled by political authorities. Faced with a rival source of influence, rulers in previous centuries had few qualms about eliminating those rare individuals who truly understood how to marshal forces that heads of state have never been able to monopolize, such as cleverly crafted language, strategically placed information, and, most important, psychological insight.

It would perhaps be expressing too much faith in human nature to claim that persuasion experts no longer face a threat from those who wield political power. But because the truth about persuasion is no longer the sole possession of a few brilliant, inspired individuals, experts in the field can presumably breathe a little easier. Indeed, since most people in power are interested in remaining in power, they're likely to be more interested in acquiring persuasion skills than abolishing them.

---

people actually do, it can't be beaten. For instance, when the news media present an acknowledged expert's views on a topic, the effect on public opinion is dramatic. A single expert-opinion news story in the *New York Times* is associated with a 2% shift in public opinion nationwide, according to a 1993 study described in the *Public Opinion Quarterly.* And researchers writing in the *American Political Science Review* in 1987 found that when the expert's view was aired on national television, public opinion shifted as much as 4%. A cynic might argue that these findings only illustrate the docile submissiveness of the public. But a fairer explanation is that, amid the teeming complexity of contemporary life, a well-selected expert offers a valuable and efficient shortcut to good decisions. Indeed, some questions, be they legal, financial, medical, or technological, require so much specialized knowledge to answer, we have no choice but to rely on experts.

Since there's good reason to defer to experts, executives should take pains to ensure that they establish their own expertise before they attempt to exert influence. Surprisingly often, people mistakenly assume that others recognize and appreciate their experience.

That's what happened at a hospital where some colleagues and I were consulting. The physical therapy staffers were frustrated because so many of their stroke patients abandoned their exercise routines as soon as they left the hospital. No matter how often the staff emphasized the importance of regular home exercise—it is, in fact, crucial to the process of regaining independent function—the message just didn't sink in.

Interviews with some of the patients helped us pinpoint the problem. They were familiar with the background and training of their physicians, but the patients knew little about the credentials of the physical therapists who were urging them to exercise. It was a simple matter to remedy that lack of information: We merely asked the therapy director to display all the awards, diplomas, and certifications of her staff on the walls of the therapy rooms. The result was startling: Exercise compliance jumped 34% and has never dropped since.

What we found immensely gratifying was not just how much we increased compliance, but how. We didn't fool or browbeat any of the patients. We *informed* them into compliance. Nothing had to be invented; no time or resources had to be spent in the process. The staff's expertise was real—all we had to do was make it more visible.

The task for managers who want to establish their claims to expertise is somewhat more difficult. They can't simply nail their diplomas to the wall and wait for everyone to notice. A little subtlety is called for. Outside the United States, it is customary for people to spend time interacting socially before getting down to business for the first time. Frequently they gather for dinner the night before their meeting or negotiation. These get-togethers can make discussions easier and help blunt disagreements—remember the findings about liking and similarity—and they can also provide an opportunity to establish expertise. Perhaps it's a matter of telling an anecdote about successfully solving a problem similar to the one that's on the agenda at the next day's meeting. Or perhaps dinner is the time to describe years spent mastering a complex discipline—not in a boastful way but as part of the ordinary give-and-take of conversation.

Granted, there's not always time for lengthy introductory sessions. But even in the course of the preliminary conversation that precedes most meetings, there is almost always an opportunity to touch lightly on your relevant background and experience as a natural part of a sociable exchange. This initial disclosure of personal information gives you a chance to establish expertise early in the game, so that when the discussion turns to the business at hand, what you have to say will be accorded the respect it deserves.

The Principle of Scarcity

People want more of what they can have less of.

The application
Highlight unique benefits and exclusive information.

Study after study shows that items and opportunities are seen to be more valuable as they become less available. That's a tremendously useful piece of information for managers. They can harness the scarcity principle with the organizational equivalents of limited-time, limited-supply, and one-of-a-kind offers. Honestly informing a coworker of a closing window of opportunity— the chance to get the boss's ear before she leaves for an extended vacation, perhaps—can mobilize action dramatically.

Managers can learn from retailers how to frame their offers not in terms of what people stand to gain but in terms of what they stand to lose if they don't act on the information. The power of "loss language" was demonstrated in a 1988 study of California home owners written up in the *Journal of Applied Psychology*. Half were told that if they fully insulated their homes, they would save a certain amount of money each day. The other half were told that if they failed to insulate, they would lose that amount each day. Significantly more people insulated their homes when exposed to the loss language. The same phenomenon occurs in business. According to a 1994 study in the journal *Organizational Behavior and Human Decision*

Processes, potential losses figure far more heavily in managers' decision making than potential gains.

In framing their offers, executives should also remember that exclusive information is more persuasive than widely available data. A doctoral student of mine, Amram Knishinsky, wrote his 1982 dissertation on the purchase decisions of wholesale beef buyers. He observed that they more than doubled their orders when they were told that, because of certain weather conditions overseas, there was likely to be a scarcity of foreign beef in the near future. But their orders increased 600% when they were informed that no one else had that information yet.

The persuasive power of exclusivity can be harnessed by any manager who comes into possession of information that's not broadly available and that supports an idea or initiative he or she would like the organization to adopt. The next time that kind of information crosses your desk, round up your organization's key players. The information itself may seem dull, but exclusivity will give it a special sheen. Push it across your desk and say, "I just got this report today. It won't be distributed until next week, but I want to give you an early look at what it shows." Then watch your listeners lean forward.

Allow me to stress here a point that should be obvious. No offer of exclusive information, no exhortation to act now or miss this opportunity forever should be made unless it is genuine. Deceiving colleagues into compliance is not only ethically objectionable, it's foolhardy. If the deception is detected—and it certainly will be—it will snuff out any enthusiasm the offer originally kindled. It will also invite dishonesty toward the deceiver. Remember the rule of reciprocity.

Putting It All Together

There's nothing abstruse or obscure about these six principles of persuasion. Indeed, they neatly codify our intuitive understanding of the ways people evaluate information and form decisions. As a result, the principles are easy for most people to grasp, even those with no formal education in psychology. But in the seminars and workshops I conduct, I have learned that two points bear repeated emphasis.

First, although the six principles and their applications can be discussed separately for the sake of clarity, they should be applied in combination to compound their impact. For instance, in discussing the importance of expertise, I suggested that managers use informal, social conversations to establish their credentials. But that conversation affords an opportunity to gain information as well as convey it. While you're showing your dinner companion that you have the skills and experience your business problem demands, you can also learn about your companion's background, likes, and dislikes—information that will help you locate genuine similarities and give sincere compliments. By letting your expertise surface and also establishing rapport, you double your persuasive power. And if you succeed in bringing your dinner partner on board, you may encourage other people to sign on as well, thanks to the persuasive power of social evidence.

The other point I wish to emphasize is that the rules of ethics apply to the science of social influence just as they do to any other technology. Not only is it ethically wrong to trick or trap others into assent, it's ill-advised in practical terms. Dishonest or high-pressure tactics work only in the short run, if at all. Their long-term effects are malignant, especially within an organization, which can't function properly without a bedrock level of trust and cooperation.

That point is made vividly in the following account, which a department head for a large textile manufacturer related at a training workshop I conducted. She described a vice president in her company who wrung public commitments from department heads in a highly manipulative manner. Instead of giving his subordinates time to talk or think through his proposals carefully, he would approach them individually at the busiest moment of their workday and describe the benefits of his plan in exhaustive, patience-straining detail. Then he would move in for the kill. "It's very important for me to see you as being on my team on this," he would say. "Can I count on your support?" Intimidated, frazzled, eager to chase the man from their offices so they could get back to work, the department heads would invariably go along with his request. But because the commitments never felt voluntary, the department heads never followed through, and as a result the vice president's initiatives all blew up or petered out.

This story had a deep impact on the other participants in the workshop. Some gulped in shock as they recognized their own manipulative behavior. But what stopped everyone cold was the expression on the department head's face as she recounted the damaging collapse of her superior's proposals. She was smiling.

Nothing I could say would more effectively make the point that the deceptive or coercive use of the principles of social influence is ethically wrong and pragmatically wrongheaded. Yet the same principles, if applied appropriately, can steer decisions correctly. Legitimate expertise, genuine obligations, authentic similarities, real social proof, exclusive news, and freely made commitments can produce choices that are likely to benefit both parties. And any approach that works to everyone's mutual benefit is good business, don't you think? Of course, I don't want to press you into it, but, if you agree, I would love it if you could just jot me a memo to that effect.

Originally published in September 2001. Reprint R0109D

The Power of Talk

Who Gets Heard and Why.

by Deborah Tannen

THE HEAD OF A LARGE division of a multinational corporation was running a meeting devoted to performance assessment. Each senior manager stood up, reviewed the individuals in his group, and evaluated them for promotion. Although there were women in every group, not one of them made the cut. One after another, each manager declared, in effect, that every woman in his group didn't have the self-confidence needed to be promoted. The division head began to doubt his ears. How could it be that all the talented women in the division suffered from a lack of self-confidence?

In all likelihood, they didn't. Consider the many women who have left large corporations to start their own businesses, obviously exhibiting enough confidence to succeed on their own. Judgments about confidence can be inferred only from the way people present themselves, and much of that presentation is in the form of talk.

The CEO of a major corporation told me that he often has to make decisions in five minutes about matters on which others may have worked five months. He said he uses this rule: If the person making the proposal seems confident, the CEO approves it. If not, he says no. This might seem like a reasonable approach. But my field of research, sociolinguistics, suggests otherwise. The CEO obviously thinks he knows what a confident person sounds like. But his judgment, which may be dead right for some people, may be dead wrong for others.

Communication isn't as simple as saying what you mean. How you say what you mean is crucial, and differs from one person to the next, because using language is learned social behavior: How we talk and listen are deeply influenced by cultural experience. Although we might think that our ways of saying what we mean are natural, we can run into trouble if we interpret and evaluate others as if they necessarily felt the same way we'd feel if we spoke the way they did.

Since 1974, I have been researching the influence of linguistic style on conversations and human relationships. In the past four years, I have extended that research to the workplace, where I have observed how ways of speaking learned in childhood affect judgments of competence and confidence, as well as who gets heard, who gets credit, and what gets done.

The division head who was dumbfounded to hear that all the talented women in his organization lacked confidence was probably right to be skeptical. The senior managers were judging the women in their groups by their own linguistic norms, but women—like people who have grown up in a different culture—have often learned different styles of speaking than men, which can make them seem less competent and self-assured than they are.

What Is Linguistic Style?

Everything that is said must be said in a certain way—in a certain tone of voice, at a certain rate of speed, and with a certain degree of loudness. Whereas often we consciously consider what to say before speaking, we rarely think about how to say it, unless the situation is obviously loaded—for example, a job interview or a tricky performance review. Linguistic style refers to a person's characteristic speaking pattern. It includes such features as directness or indirectness, pacing and pausing, word choice, and the use of such elements as jokes, figures of speech, stories, questions, and apologies. In other words, linguistic style is a set of culturally learned signals by which we not only communicate what we mean but also interpret others' meaning and evaluate one another as people.

Idea in Brief

Most managerial work happens through talk—discussions, meetings, presentations, negotiations. And it is through talk that managers evaluate others and are themselves judged. Using research carried out in a variety of workplace settings, linguist Deborah Tannen demonstrates how conversational style often overrides what we say, affecting who gets heard, who gets credit, and what gets done. Tannen's linguistic perspective provides managers with insight into why there is so much poor communication. Gender plays an important role. Tannen traces the ways in which women's styles can undermine them in the workplace, making them seem less competent, confident, and self-assured than they are. She analyzes the underlying social dynamic created through talk in common workplace interactions. She argues that a better understanding of linguistic style will make managers better listeners and more effective communicators, allowing them to develop more flexible approaches to a full range of managerial activities.

Consider turn taking, one element of linguistic style. Conversation is an enterprise in which people take turns: One person speaks, then the other responds. However, this apparently simple exchange requires a subtle negotiation of signals so that you know when the other person is finished and it's your turn to begin. Cultural factors such as country or region of origin and ethnic background influence how long a pause seems natural. When Bob, who is from Detroit, has a conversation with his colleague Joe, from New York City, it's hard for him to get a word in edgewise because he expects a slightly longer pause between turns than Joe does. A pause of that length never comes because, before it has a chance to, Joe senses an uncomfortable silence, which he fills with more talk of his own. Both men fail to realize that differences in conversational style are getting in their way. Bob thinks that Joe is pushy and uninterested in what he has to say, and Joe thinks that Bob doesn't have much to contribute. Similarly, when Sally relocated from Texas to Washington, D.C., she kept searching for the right time to break in during staff meetings—and never found it. Although in Texas she was considered outgoing and confident, in Washington she was perceived as shy and retiring. Her boss even suggested she take an assertiveness

The Idea in Practice

This table shows examples of styles of *talking* (including the *assumptions* behind each style) and *unintended consequences* a company may suffer because of misinterpreted stylistic differences.

	Style of Talking	Unintended Consequences of Style
Sharing Credit	Uses "we" rather than "I" to describe accomplishments. *Why?* Using "I" seems too self-promoting.	Speaker doesn't get credit for accomplishments and may hesitate to offer good ideas in the future.
Acting Modest	Downplays their certainty, rather than minimizing doubts, about future performance. *Why?* Confident behavior seems too boastful.	Speaker *appears* to lack confidence and, therefore, competence; others reject speaker's good ideas.
Asking Questions	Asks questions freely. *Why?* Questions generate needed knowledge.	Speaker *appears* ignorant to others; if organization discourages speaker from asking questions, valuable knowledge remains buried.

training course. Thus slight differences in conversational style—in these cases, a few seconds of pause—can have a surprising impact on who gets heard and on the judgments, including psychological ones, that are made about people and their abilities.

Every utterance functions on two levels. We're all familiar with the first one: Language communicates ideas. The second level is mostly invisible to us, but it plays a powerful role in communication. As a form of social behavior, language also negotiates relationships. Through ways of speaking, we signal—and create—the relative status of speakers and their level of rapport. If you say, "Sit down!" you

Apologizing	Apologizes freely. *Why?* Apologies express concern for others.	Speaker *appears* to lack authority.
Giving Feedback	Notes weaknesses only after *first* citing strengths. *Why?* Buffering criticism saves face for the individual receiving feedback.	Person receiving feedback concludes that areas needing improvement aren't important.
Avoiding Verbal Opposition	Avoids challenging others' ideas, and hedges when stating own ideas. *Why?* Verbal opposition signals destructive fighting.	Others conclude that speaker has weak ideas.
Managing Up	Avoids talking up achievements with higher-ups. *Why?* Emphasizing achievements to higher-ups constitutes boasting.	Managers conclude that speaker hasn't achieved much and doesn't deserve recognition or promotion.
Being Indirect	Speaks indirectly rather than bluntly when telling subordinates what to do. *Why?* Blatantly directing others is too bossy.	Subordinates conclude that manager lacks assertiveness and clear thinking, and judge manager's directives as unimportant.

are signaling that you have higher status than the person you are addressing, that you are so close to each other that you can drop all pleasantries, or that you are angry. If you say, "I would be honored if you would sit down," you are signaling great respect—or great sarcasm, depending on your tone of voice, the situation, and what you both know about how close you really are. If you say, "You must be so tired—why don't you sit down," you are communicating either closeness and concern or condescension. Each of these ways of saying "the same thing"—telling someone to sit down—can have a vastly different meaning.

In every community known to linguists, the patterns that constitute linguistic style are relatively different for men and women. What's "natural" for most men speaking a given language is, in some cases, different from what's "natural" for most women. That is because we learn ways of speaking as children growing up, especially from peers, and children tend to play with other children of the same sex. The research of sociologists, anthropologists, and psychologists observing American children at play has shown that, although both girls and boys find ways of creating rapport and negotiating status, girls tend to learn conversational rituals that focus on the rapport dimension of relationships whereas boys tend to learn rituals that focus on the status dimension.

Girls tend to play with a single best friend or in small groups, and they spend a lot of time talking. They use language to negotiate how close they are; for example, the girl you tell your secrets to becomes your best friend. Girls learn to downplay ways in which one is better than the others and to emphasize ways in which they are all the same. From childhood, most girls learn that sounding too sure of themselves will make them unpopular with their peers—although nobody really takes such modesty literally. A group of girls will ostracize a girl who calls attention to her own superiority and criticize her by saying, "She thinks she's something"; and a girl who tells others what to do is called "bossy." Thus girls learn to talk in ways that balance their own needs with those of others—to save face for one another in the broadest sense of the term.

Boys tend to play very differently. They usually play in larger groups in which more boys can be included, but not everyone is treated as an equal. Boys with high status in their group are expected to emphasize rather than downplay their status, and usually one or several boys will be seen as the leader or leaders. Boys generally don't accuse one another of being bossy, because the leader is expected to tell lower-status boys what to do. Boys learn to use language to negotiate their status in the group by displaying their abilities and knowledge, and by challenging others and resisting challenges. Giving orders is one way of getting and keeping the high-status role. Another is taking center stage by telling stories or jokes.

This is not to say that all boys and girls grow up this way or feel comfortable in these groups or are equally successful at negotiating within these norms. But, for the most part, these childhood play groups are where boys and girls learn their conversational styles. In this sense, they grow up in different worlds. The result is that women and men tend to have different habitual ways of saying what they mean, and conversations between them can be like cross-cultural communication: You can't assume that the other person means what you would mean if you said the same thing in the same way.

My research in companies across the United States shows that the lessons learned in childhood carry over into the workplace. Consider the following example: A focus group was organized at a major multinational company to evaluate a recently implemented flextime policy. The participants sat in a circle and discussed the new system. The group concluded that it was excellent, but they also agreed on ways to improve it. The meeting went well and was deemed a success by all, according to my own observations and everyone's comments to me. But the next day, I was in for a surprise.

I had left the meeting with the impression that Phil had been responsible for most of the suggestions adopted by the group. But as I typed up my notes, I noticed that Cheryl had made almost all those suggestions. I had thought that the key ideas came from Phil because he had picked up Cheryl's points and supported them, speaking at greater length in doing so than she had in raising them.

It would be easy to regard Phil as having stolen Cheryl's ideas—and her thunder. But that would be inaccurate. Phil never claimed Cheryl's ideas as his own. Cheryl herself told me later that she left the meeting confident that she had contributed significantly, and that she appreciated Phil's support. She volunteered, with a laugh, "It was not one of those times when a woman says something and it's ignored, then a man says it and it's picked up." In other words, Cheryl and Phil worked well as a team, the group fulfilled its charge, and the company got what it needed. So what was the problem?

I went back and asked all the participants who they thought had been the most influential group member, the one most responsible for the ideas that had been adopted. The pattern of answers was revealing. The two other women in the group named Cheryl. Two of the three men named Phil. Of the men, only Phil named Cheryl. In other words, in this instance, the women evaluated the contribution of another woman more accurately than the men did.

Meetings like this take place daily in companies around the country. Unless managers are unusually good at listening closely to how people say what they mean, the talents of someone like Cheryl may well be undervalued and underutilized.

One Up, One Down

Individual speakers vary in how sensitive they are to the social dynamics of language—in other words, to the subtle nuances of what others say to them. Men tend to be sensitive to the power dynamics of interaction, speaking in ways that position themselves as one up and resisting being put in a one-down position by others. Women tend to react more strongly to the rapport dynamic, speaking in ways that save face for others and buffering statements that could be seen as putting others in a one-down position. These linguistic patterns are pervasive; you can hear them in hundreds of exchanges in the workplace every day. And, as in the case of Cheryl and Phil, they affect who gets heard and who gets credit.

Getting credit. Even so small a linguistic strategy as the choice of pronoun can affect who gets credit. In my research in the workplace, I heard men say "I" in situations where I heard women say "we." For example, one publishing company executive said, "I'm hiring a new manager. I'm going to put him in charge of my marketing division," as if he owned the corporation. In stark contrast, I recorded women saying "we" when referring to work they alone had done. One woman explained that it would sound too self-promoting to claim credit in an obvious way by saying, "I did this." Yet she expected—sometimes vainly—that others would know it was her work and would give her the credit she did not claim for herself.

Managers might leap to the conclusion that women who do not take credit for what they've done should be taught to do so. But that solution is problematic because we associate ways of speaking with moral qualities: The way we speak is who we are and who we want to be.

Veronica, a senior researcher in a high-tech company, had an observant boss. He noticed that many of the ideas coming out of the group were hers but that often someone else trumpeted them around the office and got credit for them. He advised her to "own" her ideas and make sure she got the credit. But Veronica found she simply didn't enjoy her work if she had to approach it as what seemed to her an unattractive and unappealing "grabbing game." It was her dislike of such behavior that had led her to avoid it in the first place.

Whatever the motivation, women are less likely than men to have learned to blow their own horn. And they are more likely than men to believe that if they do so, they won't be liked.

Many have argued that the growing trend of assigning work to teams may be especially congenial to women, but it may also create complications for performance evaluation. When ideas are generated and work is accomplished in the privacy of the team, the outcome of the team's effort may become associated with the person most vocal about reporting results. There are many women and men—but probably relatively more women—who are reluctant to put themselves forward in this way and who consequently risk not getting credit for their contributions.

Confidence and boasting

The CEO who based his decisions on the confidence level of speakers was articulating a value that is widely shared in U.S. businesses: One way to judge confidence is by an individual's behavior, especially verbal behavior. Here again, many women are at a disadvantage.

Studies show that women are more likely to downplay their certainty and men are more likely to minimize their doubts. Psychologist Laurie Heatherington and her colleagues devised an ingenious experiment, which they reported in the journal *Sex Roles* (Volume 29, 1993). They asked hundreds of incoming college students to predict what grades they would get in their first year. Some subjects were asked to make their predictions privately by writing them down and placing them in an envelope; others were asked to make their predictions publicly, in the presence of a researcher. The results showed that more women than men predicted lower grades for themselves if they made their predictions publicly. If they made their predictions privately, the predictions were the same as those of the men—and the same as their actual grades. This study provides evidence that what comes across as lack of confidence—predicting lower grades for oneself—may reflect not one's actual level of confidence but the desire not to seem boastful.

These habits with regard to appearing humble or confident result from the socialization of boys and girls by their peers in childhood play. As adults, both women and men find these behaviors reinforced by the positive responses they get from friends and relatives who share the same norms. But the norms of behavior in the U.S. business world are based on the style of interaction that is more common among men—at least, among American men.

Asking questions

Although asking the right questions is one of the hallmarks of a good manager, how and when questions are asked can send unintended signals about competence and power. In a group, if only one person asks questions, he or she risks being seen as the only ignorant one. Furthermore, we judge others not only by how they speak but also by how they are spoken to. The person who asks questions may end up being lectured to and looking like a novice under a schoolmaster's tutelage. The way boys are socialized makes them more likely to be aware of the underlying power dynamic by which a question asker can be seen in a one-down position.

One practicing physician learned the hard way that any exchange of information can become the basis for judgments—or misjudgments—about competence. During her training, she received a negative evaluation that she thought was unfair, so she asked her supervising physician for an explanation. He said that she knew less than her peers. Amazed at his answer, she asked how he had reached that conclusion. He said, "You ask more questions."

Along with cultural influences and individual personality, gender seems to play a role in whether and when people ask questions. For example, of all the observations I've made in lectures and books, the one that sparks the most enthusiastic flash of recognition is that men are less likely than women to stop and ask for directions when they are lost. I explain that men often resist asking for directions because they are aware that it puts them in a one-down position and because they value the independence that comes with finding their way by themselves. Asking for directions while driving is only one instance—along with many others that researchers have examined—in which men seem less likely than women to ask questions. I believe this is because they are more attuned than women to the potential face-losing aspect of asking questions. And men who believe that asking questions might reflect negatively on them may, in turn, be likely to form a negative opinion of others who ask questions in situations where they would not.

Conversational Rituals

Conversation is fundamentally ritual in the sense that we speak in ways our culture has conventionalized and expect certain types of responses. Take greetings, for example. I have heard visitors to the United States complain that Americans are hypocritical because they ask how you are but aren't interested in the answer. To Americans, How are you? is obviously a ritualized way to start a conversation rather than a literal request for information. In other parts of the world, including the Philippines, people ask each other, "Where are you going?" when they meet. The question seems intrusive to Americans, who do not realize that it, too, is a ritual query to which the only expected reply is a vague "Over there."

It's easy and entertaining to observe different rituals in foreign countries. But we don't expect differences, and are far less likely to recognize the ritualized nature of our conversations, when we are with our compatriots at work. Our differing rituals can be even more problematic when we think we're all speaking the same language.

Apologies

Consider the simple phrase *I'm sorry*.

Catherine: How did that big presentation go?

Bob: Oh, not very well. I got a lot of flak from the VP for finance, and I didn't have the numbers at my fingertips.

Catherine: Oh, I'm sorry. I know how hard you worked on that.

In this case, *I'm sorry* probably means "I'm sorry that happened," not "I apologize," unless it was Catherine's responsibility to supply Bob with the numbers for the presentation. Women tend to say *I'm sorry* more frequently than men, and often they intend it in this way—as a ritualized means of expressing concern. It's one of many learned elements of conversational style that girls often use to establish rapport. Ritual apologies—like other conversational rituals—work well when both parties share the same assumptions about their use. But people who utter frequent ritual apologies may end up appearing weaker, less confident, and literally more blameworthy than people who don't.

Apologies tend to be regarded differently by men, who are more likely to focus on the status implications of exchanges. Many men avoid apologies because they see them as putting the speaker in a one-down position. I observed with some amazement an encounter among several lawyers engaged in a negotiation over a speakerphone. At one point, the lawyer in whose office I was sitting accidentally elbowed the telephone and cut off the call. When his secretary got the parties back on again, I expected him to say what I would have said: "Sorry about that. I knocked the phone with my elbow." Instead, he said, "Hey, what happened? One minute you were there; the next minute you were gone!" This lawyer seemed to have an automatic impulse not to admit fault if he didn't have to. For me, it was one of those pivotal moments when you realize that the world you live in is not the one everyone lives in and that the way you assume is the way to talk is really only one of many.

Those who caution managers not to undermine their authority by apologizing are approaching interaction from the perspective of the power dynamic. In many cases, this strategy is effective. On the other hand, when I asked people what frustrated them in their jobs, one frequently voiced complaint was working with or for someone who refuses to apologize or admit fault. In other words, accepting responsibility for errors and admitting mistakes may be an equally effective or superior strategy in some settings.

Feedback

Styles of giving feedback contain a ritual element that often is the cause for misunderstanding. Consider the following exchange: A manager had to tell her marketing director to rewrite a report. She began this potentially awkward task by citing the report's strengths and then moved to the main point: the weaknesses that needed to be remedied. The marketing director seemed to understand and accept his supervisor's comments, but his revision contained only minor changes and failed to address the major weaknesses. When the manager told him of her dissatisfaction, he accused her of misleading him: "You told me it was fine."

The impasse resulted from different linguistic styles. To the manager, it was natural to buffer the criticism by beginning with praise. Telling her subordinate that his report is inadequate and has to be rewritten puts him in a one-down position. Praising him for the parts that are good is a ritualized way of saving face for him. But the marketing director did not share his supervisor's assumption about how feedback should be given. Instead, he assumed that what she mentioned first was the main point and that what she brought up later was an afterthought.

Those who expect feedback to come in the way the manager presented it would appreciate her tact and would regard a more blunt approach as unnecessarily callous. But those who share the marketing director's assumptions would regard the blunt approach as honest and no-nonsense, and the manager's as obfuscating. Because each one's assumptions seemed self-evident, each blamed the other: The manager thought the marketing director was not listening, and he thought she had not communicated clearly or had changed her mind. This is significant because it illustrates that incidents labeled vaguely as "poor communication" may be the result of differing linguistic styles.

Compliments

Exchanging compliments is a common ritual, especially among women. A mismatch in expectations about this ritual left Susan, a manager in the human resources field, in a one-down position. She and her colleague Bill had both given presentations at a national conference. On the airplane home, Susan told Bill, "That was a great talk!" "Thank you," he said. Then she asked, "What did you think of mine?" He responded with a lengthy and detailed critique, as she listened uncomfortably. An unpleasant feeling of having been put down came over her. Somehow she had been positioned as the novice in need of his expert advice. Even worse, she had only herself to blame, since she had, after all, asked Bill what he thought of her talk.

But had Susan asked for the response she received? When she asked Bill what he thought about her talk, she expected to hear not a critique but a compliment. In fact, her question had been an attempt to repair a ritual gone awry. Susan's initial compliment to Bill was the kind of automatic recognition she felt was more or less required after a colleague gives a presentation, and she expected Bill to respond with a matching compliment. She was just talking automatically, but he either sincerely misunderstood the ritual or simply took the opportunity to bask in the one-up position of critic. Whatever his motivation, it was Susan's attempt to spark an exchange of compliments that gave him the opening.

Although this exchange could have occurred between two men, it does not seem coincidental that it happened between a man and a woman. Linguist Janet Holmes discovered that women pay more compliments than men (*Anthropological Linguistics,* Volume 28, 1986). And, as I have observed, fewer men are likely to ask, "What did you think of my talk?" precisely because the question might invite an unwanted critique.

In the social structure of the peer groups in which they grow up, boys are indeed looking for opportunities to put others down and take the one-up position for themselves. In contrast, one of the rituals girls learn is taking the one-down position but assuming that the other person will recognize the ritual nature of the self-denigration and pull them back up.

The exchange between Susan and Bill also suggests how women's and men's characteristic styles may put women at a disadvantage in the workplace. If one person is trying to minimize status differences, maintain an appearance that everyone is equal, and save face for the other, while another person is trying to maintain the one-up position and avoid being positioned as one down, the person seeking the one-up position is likely to get it. At the same time, the person who has not been expending any effort to avoid the one-down position is likely to end up in it. Because women are more likely to take (or accept) the role of advice seeker, men are more inclined to interpret a ritual question from a woman as a request for advice.

Ritual opposition

Apologizing, mitigating criticism with praise, and exchanging compliments are rituals common among women that men often take literally. A ritual common among men that women often take literally is ritual opposition.

A woman in communications told me she watched with distaste and distress as her office mate argued heatedly with another colleague about whose division should suffer budget cuts. She was even more surprised, however, that a short time later they were as friendly as ever. "How can you pretend that fight never happened?" she asked. "Who's pretending it never happened?" he responded, as puzzled by her question as she had been by his behavior. "It happened," he said, "and it's over." What she took as literal fighting to him was a routine part of daily negotiation: a ritual fight.

Many Americans expect the discussion of ideas to be a ritual fight—that is, an exploration through verbal opposition. They present their own ideas in the most certain and absolute form they can, and wait to see if they are challenged. Being forced to defend an idea provides an opportunity to test it. In the same spirit, they may play devil's advocate in challenging their colleagues' ideas—trying to poke holes and find weaknesses—as a way of helping them explore and test their ideas.

This style can work well if everyone shares it, but those unaccustomed to it are likely to miss its ritual nature. They may give up an idea that is challenged, taking the objections as an indication that the idea was a poor one. Worse, they may take the opposition as a personal attack and may find it impossible to do their best in a contentious environment. People unaccustomed to this style may hedge when stating their ideas in order to fend off potential attacks. Ironically, this posture makes their arguments appear weak and is more likely to invite attack from pugnacious colleagues than to fend it off.

Ritual opposition can even play a role in who gets hired. Some consulting firms that recruit graduates from the top business schools use a confrontational interviewing technique. They challenge the candidate to "crack a case" in real time. A partner at one firm told me, "Women tend to do less well in this kind of interaction, and it certainly affects who gets hired. But, in fact, many women who don't 'test well' turn out to be good consultants. They're often smarter than some of the men who looked like analytic powerhouses under pressure."

The level of verbal opposition varies from one company's culture to the next, but I saw instances of it in all the organizations I studied. Anyone who is uncomfortable with this linguistic style—and that includes some men as well as many women—risks appearing insecure about his or her ideas.

Negotiating Authority

In organizations, formal authority comes from the position one holds. But actual authority has to be negotiated day to day. The effectiveness of individual managers depends in part on their skill in negotiating authority and on whether others reinforce or undercut their efforts. The way linguistic style reflects status plays a subtle role in placing individuals within a hierarchy.

Managing up and down

In all the companies I researched, I heard from women who knew they were doing a superior job and knew that their co-workers (and sometimes their immediate bosses) knew it as well, but believed that the higher-ups did not. They frequently told me that something outside themselves was holding them back and found it frustrating because they thought that all that should be necessary for success was to do a great job, that superior performance should be recognized and rewarded. In contrast, men often told me that if women weren't promoted, it was because they simply weren't up to snuff. Looking around, however, I saw evidence that men more often than women behaved in ways likely to get them recognized by those with the power to determine their advancement.

In all the companies I visited, I observed what happened at lunchtime. I saw young men who regularly ate lunch with their boss, and senior men who ate with the big boss. I noticed far fewer women who sought out the highest-level person they could eat with. But one is more likely to get recognition for work done if one talks about it to those higher up, and it is easier to do so if the lines of communication are already open. Furthermore, given the opportunity for a conversation with superiors, men and women are likely to have different ways of talking about their accomplishments because of the different ways in which they were socialized as children. Boys are rewarded by their peers if they talk up their achievements, whereas girls are rewarded if they play theirs down. Linguistic styles common among men may tend to give them some advantages when it comes to managing up.

All speakers are aware of the status of the person they are talking to and adjust accordingly. Everyone speaks differently when talking to a boss than when talking to a subordinate. But, surprisingly, the ways in which they adjust their talk may be different and thus may project different images of themselves.

Communications researchers Karen Tracy and Eric Eisenberg studied how relative status affects the way people give criticism. They devised a business letter that contained some errors and asked

13 male and 11 female college students to role-play delivering criticism under two scenarios. In the first, the speaker was a boss talking to a subordinate; in the second, the speaker was a subordinate talking to his or her boss. The researchers measured how hard the speakers tried to avoid hurting the feelings of the person they were criticizing.

One might expect people to be more careful about how they deliver criticism when they are in a subordinate position. Tracy and Eisenberg found that hypothesis to be true for the men in their study but not for the women. As they reported in *Research on Language and Social Interaction* (Volume 24, 1990/1991), the women showed more concern about the other person's feelings when they were playing the role of superior. In other words, the women were more careful to save face for the other person when they were managing down than when they were managing up. This pattern recalls the way girls are socialized: Those who are in some way superior are expected to downplay rather than flaunt their superiority.

In my own recordings of workplace communication, I observed women talking in similar ways. For example, when a manager had to correct a mistake made by her secretary, she did so by acknowledging that there were mitigating circumstances. She said, laughing, "You know, it's hard to do things around here, isn't it, with all these people coming in!" The manager was saving face for her subordinate, just like the female students role-playing in the Tracy and Eisenberg study.

Is this an effective way to communicate? One must ask, effective for what? The manager in question established a positive environment in her group, and the work was done effectively. On the other hand, numerous women in many different fields told me that their bosses say they don't project the proper authority.

Indirectness

Another linguistic signal that varies with power and status is indirectness—the tendency to say what we mean without spelling it out in so many words. Despite the widespread belief in the United States that it's always best to say exactly what we mean, indirectness is a fundamental and pervasive element in human communication. It also is one of the elements that vary most from one culture to another, and it can cause enormous misunderstanding when speakers have different habits and expectations about how it is used. It's often said that American women are more indirect than American men, but in fact everyone tends to be indirect in some situations and in different ways. Allowing for cultural, ethnic, regional, and individual differences, women are especially likely to be indirect when it comes to telling others what to do, which is not surprising, considering girls' readiness to brand other girls as bossy. On the other hand, men are especially likely to be indirect when it comes to admitting fault or weakness, which also is not surprising, considering boys' readiness to push around boys who assume the one-down position.

At first glance, it would seem that only the powerful can get away with bald commands such as, "Have that report on my desk by noon." But power in an organization also can lead to requests so indirect that they don't sound like requests at all. A boss who says, "Do we have the sales data by product line for each region?" would be surprised and frustrated if a subordinate responded, "We probably do" rather than "I'll get it for you."

Examples such as these notwithstanding, many researchers have claimed that those in subordinate positions are more likely to speak indirectly, and that is surely accurate in some situations. For example, linguist Charlotte Linde, in a study published in *Language in Society* (Volume 17, 1988), examined the black-box conversations that took place between pilots and copilots before airplane crashes. In one particularly tragic instance, an Air Florida plane crashed into the Potomac River immediately after attempting takeoff from National Airport in Washington, D.C., killing all but 5 of the 74 people on board. The pilot, it turned out, had little experience flying in icy weather. The copilot had a bit more, and it became heartbreakingly clear on analysis that he had tried to warn the pilot but had done so indirectly. Alerted by Linde's observation, I examined the transcript of the conversations and found evidence of her hypothesis. The copilot repeatedly called attention to the bad weather and to ice buildup on other planes:

> *Copilot:* Look how the ice is just hanging on his, ah, back, back there, see that? See all those icicles on the back there and everything?

> *Pilot:* Yeah.
> [The copilot also expressed concern about the long waiting time since deicing.]

> *Copilot:* Boy, this is a, this is a losing battle here on trying to deice those things; it [gives] you a false feeling of security, that's all that does.
> [Just before they took off, the copilot expressed another concern— about abnormal instrument readings—but again he didn't press the matter when it wasn't picked up by the pilot.]

> *Copilot:* That don't seem right, does it? [3-second pause]. Ah, that's not right. Well—

> *Pilot:* Yes it is, there's 80.

> *Copilot:* Naw, I don't think that's right. [7-second pause] Ah, maybe it is.

Shortly thereafter, the plane took off, with tragic results. In other instances as well as this one, Linde observed that copilots, who are second in command, are more likely to express themselves indirectly or otherwise mitigate, or soften, their communication when they are suggesting courses of action to the pilot. In an effort to avert similar disasters, some airlines now offer training for copilots to express themselves in more assertive ways.

This solution seems self-evidently appropriate to most Americans. But when I assigned Linde's article in a graduate seminar I taught, a Japanese student pointed out that it would be just as effective to train pilots to pick up on hints. This approach reflects assumptions about communication that typify Japanese culture, which places great value on the ability of people to understand one another without putting everything into words. Either directness or indirectness can be a successful means of communication as long as the linguistic style is understood by the participants.

In the world of work, however, there is more at stake than whether the communication is understood. People in powerful positions are likely to reward styles similar to their own, because we all tend to take as self-evident the logic of our own styles. Accordingly, there is evidence that in the U.S. workplace, where instructions from a superior are expected to be voiced in a relatively direct manner, those who tend to be indirect when telling subordinates what to do may be perceived as lacking in confidence.

Consider the case of the manager at a national magazine who was responsible for giving assignments to reporters. She tended to phrase her assignments as questions. For example, she asked, "How would you like to do the X project with Y?" or said, "I was thinking of putting you on the X project. Is that okay?" This worked extremely well with her staff; they liked working for her, and the work got done in an efficient and orderly manner. But when she had her midyear evaluation with her own boss, he criticized her for not assuming the proper demeanor with her staff.

In any work environment, the higher-ranking person has the power to enforce his or her view of appropriate demeanor, created in part by linguistic style. In most U.S. contexts, that view is likely to assume that the person in authority has the right to be relatively direct rather than to mitigate orders. There also are cases, however, in which the higher-ranking person assumes a more indirect style. The owner of a retail operation told her subordinate, a store manager, to do something. He said he would do it, but a week later he still hadn't. They were able to trace the difficulty to the following conversation: She had said, "The bookkeeper needs help with the billing. How would you feel about helping her out?" He had said, "Fine." This conversation had seemed to be clear and flawless at the time, but it turned out that they had interpreted this simple exchange in very different ways. She thought he meant, "Fine, I'll help the bookkeeper out." He thought he meant, "Fine, I'll think about how I would feel about helping the bookkeeper out." He did think about it and came to the conclusion that he had more important things to do and couldn't spare the time.

To the owner, "How would you feel about helping the bookkeeper out?" was an obviously appropriate way to give the order "Help the bookkeeper out with the billing." Those who expect orders to be given as bald imperatives may find such locutions annoying or even misleading. But those for whom this style is natural do not think they are being indirect. They believe they are being clear in a polite or respectful way.

What is atypical in this example is that the person with the more indirect style was the boss, so the store manager was motivated to adapt to her style. She still gives orders the same way, but the store manager now understands how she means what she says. It's more common in U.S. business contexts for the highest-ranking people to take a more direct style, with the result that many women in authority risk being judged by their superiors as lacking the appropriate demeanor—and, consequently, lacking confidence.

What to Do?

I am often asked, What is the best way to give criticism? or What is the best way to give orders?—in other words, What is the best way to communicate? The answer is that there is no one best way. The results of a given way of speaking will vary depending on the situation, the culture of the company, the relative rank of speakers, their linguistic styles, and how those styles interact with one another. Because of all those influences, any way of speaking could be perfect for communicating with one person in one situation and disastrous with someone else in another. The critical skill for managers is to become aware of the workings and power of linguistic style, to make sure that people with something valuable to contribute get heard.

It may seem, for example, that running a meeting in an unstructured way gives equal opportunity to all. But awareness of the differences in conversational style makes it easy to see the potential for unequal access. Those who are comfortable speaking up in groups, who need little or no silence before raising their hands, or who speak out easily without waiting to be recognized are far more likely to get heard at meetings. Those who refrain from talking until it's clear that the previous speaker is finished, who wait to be recognized, and who are inclined to link their comments to those of others will do fine at a meeting where everyone else is following the same rules but will have a hard time getting heard in a meeting with people whose styles are more like the first pattern. Given the socialization typical of boys and girls, men are more likely to have learned the first style and women the second, making meetings more congenial for men than for women. It's common to observe women who participate actively in one-on-one discussions or in all-female groups but who are seldom heard in meetings with a large proportion of men. On the other hand, there are women who share the style more common among men, and they run a different risk—of being seen as too aggressive.

A manager aware of those dynamics might devise any number of ways of ensuring that everyone's ideas are heard and credited. Although no single solution will fit all contexts, managers who understand the dynamics of linguistic style can develop more adaptive and flexible approaches to running or participating in meetings, mentoring or advancing the careers of others, evaluating performance, and so on. Talk is the lifeblood of managerial work, and understanding that different people have different ways of saying what they mean will make it possible to take advantage of the talents of people with a broad range of linguistic styles. As the workplace becomes more culturally diverse and business becomes more global, managers will need to become even better at reading interactions and more flexible in adjusting their own styles to the people with whom they interact.

Originally published in September 1995. Reprint 95510

The Necessary Art of Persuasion

by Jay A. Conger

IF THERE EVER WAS A time for businesspeople to learn the fine art of persuasion, it is now. Gone are the command-and-control days of executives managing by decree. Today businesses are run largely by cross-functional teams of peers and populated by baby boomers and their Generation X offspring, who show little tolerance for unquestioned authority. Electronic communication and globalization have further eroded the traditional hierarchy, as ideas and people flow more freely than ever around organizations and as decisions get made closer to the markets. These fundamental changes, more than a decade in the making but now firmly part of the economic landscape, essentially come down to this: work today gets done in an environment where people don't just ask What should I do? but Why should I do it?

To answer this why question effectively is to persuade. Yet many businesspeople misunderstand persuasion, and more still underutilize it. The reason? Persuasion is widely perceived as a skill reserved for selling products and closing deals. It is also commonly seen as just another form of manipulation—devious and to be avoided. Certainly, persuasion can be used in selling and deal-clinching situations, and it can be misused to manipulate people. But exercised constructively and to its full potential, persuasion supersedes sales and is quite the opposite of deception. Effective persuasion becomes a negotiating and learning process through which a persuader leads colleagues to a problem's shared solution. Persuasion does indeed involve moving people to a position they don't currently hold, but not by begging or cajoling. Instead, it involves careful preparation, the proper framing of arguments, the presentation of vivid supporting evidence, and the effort to find the correct emotional match with your audience.

Effective persuasion is a difficult and time-consuming proposition, but it may also be more powerful than the command-and-control managerial model it succeeds. As AlliedSignal's CEO Lawrence Bossidy said recently, "The day when you could yell and scream and beat people into good performance is over. Today you have to appeal to them by helping them see how they can get from here to there, by establishing some credibility, and by giving them some reason and help to get there. Do all those things, and they'll knock down doors." In essence, he is describing persuasion—now more than ever, the language of business leadership.

Think for a moment of your definition of persuasion. If you are like most businesspeople I have encountered (see the sidebar "Twelve Years of Watching and Listening"), you see persuasion as a relatively straightforward process. First, you strongly state your position. Second, you outline the supporting arguments, followed by a highly assertive, data-based exposition. Finally, you enter the deal-making stage and work toward a "close." In other words, you use logic, persistence, and personal enthusiasm to get others to buy a good idea. The reality is that following this process is one surefire way to fail at persuasion. (See the sidebar "Four Ways Not to Persuade.")

What, then, constitutes effective persuasion? If persuasion is a learning and negotiating process, then in the most general terms it involves phases of discovery, preparation, and dialogue. Getting ready to persuade colleagues can take weeks or months of planning as you learn about your audience and the position you intend to argue. Before they even start to talk, effective persuaders have considered their positions from every angle. What investments in time and money will my position require from others? Is my supporting

Idea in Brief

This article defines and explains the four essential elements of persuasion. Business today is largely run by teams and populated by authority-averse baby boomers and Generation Xers. That makes persuasion more important than ever as a managerial tool. But contrary to popular belief, author Jay Conger (director of the University of Southern California's Marshall Business School's Leadership Institute) asserts, persuasion is not the same as selling an idea or convincing opponents to see things your way. It is instead a process of learning from others and negotiating a shared solution. To that end, persuasion consists of these essential elements: establishing credibility, framing to find common ground, providing vivid evidence, and connecting emotionally. Credibility grows, the author says, out of two sources: expertise and relationships. The former is a function of product or process knowledge and the latter a history of listening to and working in the best interest of others. But even if a persuader's credibility is high, his position must make sense—even more, it must appeal—to the audience. Therefore, a persuader must frame his position to illuminate its benefits to everyone who will feel its impact. Persuasion then becomes a matter of presenting evidence—but not just ordinary charts and spreadsheets. The author says the most effective persuaders use vivid—even over-the-top—stories, metaphors, and examples to make their positions come alive. Finally, good persuaders have the ability to accurately sense and respond to their audience's emotional state. Sometimes, that means they have to suppress their own emotions; at other times, they must intensify them. Persuasion can be a force for enormous good in an organization, but people must understand it for what it is: an often painstaking process that requires insight, planning, and compromise.

evidence weak in any way? Are there alternative positions I need to examine?

Dialogue happens before and during the persuasion process. Before the process begins, effective persuaders use dialogue to learn more about their audience's opinions, concerns, and perspectives. During the process, dialogue continues to be a form of learning, but it is also the beginning of the negotiation stage. You invite people to discuss, even debate, the merits of your position, and then to offer honest feedback and suggest alternative solutions. That may sound

The Idea in Practice

The process of persuasion has four steps:

1. **Establish credibility.** Your credibility grows out of two sources: **expertise** and **relationships.** If you have a history of well-informed, sound judgment, your colleagues will trust your expertise. If you've demonstrated that you can work in the best interest of others, your colleagues will have confidence in your relationships.

   If you are weak on the expertise side, bolster your position by

   • learning more through formal and informal education—for example, conversations with in-house experts

   • hiring recognized outside experts

   • launching pilot projects.

To fill in the relationship gap, try

   • meeting one-on-one with key people

   • involving like-minded coworkers who have good support with your audience.

Example: Two developers at Microsoft envisioned a controversial new software product, but both were technology novices. By working closely with technical experts and market testing a prototype, they persuaded management that the new product was ideally suited to the average computer user. It sold half a million units.

2. **Frame goals on common ground.** Tangibly describe the benefits of your position. The fastest way to get a child to the grocery store is to point out the lollipops by the cash register. That is not deception—it's

like a slow way to achieve your goal, but effective persuasion is about testing and revising ideas in concert with your colleagues' concerns and needs. In fact, the best persuaders not only listen to others but also incorporate their perspectives into a shared solution.

Persuasion, in other words, often involves—indeed, demands—compromise. Perhaps that is why the most effective persuaders seem to share a common trait: they are open-minded, never dogmatic. They enter the persuasion process prepared to adjust their viewpoints and incorporate others' ideas. That approach to persuasion. When no shared advantages are apparent, adjust your position.

Example: An ad agency executive persuaded skeptical fast-food franchisees to support headquarters' new price discounts. She cited reliable research showing how the pricing scheme improved franchisees' profits. They supported the new plan unanimously.

3. **Vividly reinforce your position.** Ordinary evidence won't do. Make numerical data more compelling with examples, stories, and metaphors that have an emotional impact.

Example: The founder of Mary Kay Cosmetics made a speech comparing sales people's weekly meetings to gatherings among Christians resisting Roman rule. This drove home the importance of a mutually supportive sales force and imbued the work with a sense of heroic mission.

4. **Connect emotionally.** Adjust your own emotional tone to match each audience's ability to receive your message. Learn how your colleagues have interpreted past events in the organization and sense how they will probably interpret your proposal. Test key individuals' possible reactions.

Example: A Chrysler team leader raised the morale of employees demoralized by foreign competition and persuaded management to bring a new car design in-house. He showed both audiences slides of his hometown, which had been devastated by foreign mining competition. His patriotic appeal reinvigorated his team, and the chairman approved the plan.

persuasion is, interestingly, highly persuasive in itself. When colleagues see that a persuader is eager to hear their views and willing to make changes in response to their needs and concerns, they respond very positively. They trust the persuader more and listen more attentively. They don't fear being bowled over or manipulated. They see the persuader as flexible and are thus more willing to make sacrifices themselves. Because that is such a powerful dynamic, good persuaders often enter the persuasion process with judicious compromises already prepared.

Twelve Years of Watching and Listening

THE IDEAS BEHIND THIS ARTICLE spring from three streams of research.

For the last 12 years as both an academic and as a consultant, I have been studying 23 senior business leaders who have shown themselves to be effective change agents. Specifically, I have investigated how these individuals use language to motivate their employees, articulate vision and strategy, and mobilize their organizations to adapt to challenging business environments.

Four years ago, I started a second stream of research exploring the capabilities and characteristics of successful cross-functional team leaders. The core of my database comprised interviews with and observations of 18 individuals working in a range of U.S. and Canadian companies. These were not senior leaders as in my earlier studies but low- and middle-level managers. Along with interviewing the colleagues of these people, I also compared their skills with those of other team leaders—in particular, with the leaders of less successful cross-functional teams engaged in similar initiatives within the same companies. Again, my focus was on language, but I also studied the influence of interpersonal skills.

The similarities in the persuasion skills possessed by both the change-agent leaders and effective team leaders prompted me to explore the academic literature on persuasion and rhetoric, as well as on the art of gospel preaching. Meanwhile, to learn how most managers approach the persuasion process, I observed several dozen managers in company meetings, and I employed simulations in company executive-education programs where groups of managers had to persuade one another on hypothetical business objectives. Finally, I selected a group of 14 managers known for their outstanding abilities in constructive persuasion. For several months, I interviewed them and their colleagues and observed them in actual work situations.

Four Essential Steps

Effective persuasion involves four distinct and essential steps. First, effective persuaders establish credibility. Second, they frame their goals in a way that identifies common ground with those they intend to persuade. Third, they reinforce their positions using vivid language and compelling evidence. And fourth, they connect emotionally with their audience. As one of the most effective executives in our research commented, "The most valuable lesson I've learned about persuasion over the years is that there's just as much strategy in how you present your position as in the position itself. In fact, I'd say the strategy of presentation is the more critical."

Establish credibility

The first hurdle persuaders must overcome is their own credibility. A persuader can't advocate a new or contrarian position without having people wonder, Can we trust this individual's perspectives and opinions? Such a reaction is understandable. After all, allowing oneself to be persuaded is risky, because any new initiative demands a commitment of time and resources. Yet even though persuaders must have high credibility, our research strongly suggests that most managers overestimate their own credibility—considerably.

In the workplace, credibility grows out of two sources: expertise and relationships. People are considered to have high levels of expertise if they have a history of sound judgment or have proven themselves knowledgeable and well informed about their proposals. For example, in proposing a new product idea, an effective persuader would need to be perceived as possessing a thorough understanding of the product—its specifications, target markets, customers, and competing products. A history of prior successes would further strengthen the persuader's perceived expertise. One extremely successful executive in our research had a track record of 14 years of devising highly effective advertising campaigns. Not surprisingly, he had an easy time winning colleagues over to his position. Another manager had a track record of seven successful new-product launches in a period of five years. He, too, had an advantage when it came to persuading his colleagues to support his next new idea.

On the relationship side, people with high credibility have demonstrated—again, usually over time—that they can be trusted to listen and to work in the best interests of others. They have also consistently shown strong emotional character and integrity; that is, they are not known for mood extremes or inconsistent performance. Indeed, people who are known to be honest, steady, and reliable have an edge when going into any persuasion situation. Because their relationships are robust, they are more apt to be given the benefit of the doubt. One effective persuader in our research was

Four Ways Not to Persuade

IN MY WORK WITH MANAGERS as a researcher and as a consultant, I have had the unfortunate opportunity to see executives fail miserably at persuasion. Here are the four most common mistakes people make:

1. **They attempt to make their case with an up-front, hard sell.** I call this the John Wayne approach. Managers strongly state their position at the outset, and then through a process of persistence, logic, and exuberance, they try to push the idea to a close. In reality, setting out a strong position at the start of a persuasion effort gives potential opponents something to grab onto—and fight against. It's far better to present your position with the finesse and reserve of a lion tamer, who engages his "partner" by showing him the legs of a chair. In other words, effective persuaders don't begin the process by giving their colleagues a clear target in which to set their jaws.

2. **They resist compromise.** Too many managers see compromise as surrender, but it is essential to constructive persuasion. Before people buy into a proposal, they want to see that the persuader is flexible enough to respond to their concerns. Compromises can often lead to better, more sustainable shared solutions.

   By not compromising, ineffective persuaders unconsciously send the message that they think persuasion is a one-way street. But persuasion

---

considered by colleagues to be remarkably trustworthy and fair; many people confided in her. In addition, she generously shared credit for good ideas and provided staff with exposure to the company's senior executives. This woman had built strong relationships, which meant her staff and peers were always willing to consider seriously what she proposed.

If expertise and relationships determine credibility, it is crucial that you undertake an honest assessment of where you stand on both criteria before beginning to persuade. To do so, first step back and ask yourself the following questions related to expertise: How will others perceive my knowledge about the strategy, product, or change I am proposing? Do I have a track record in this area that others know about and respect? Then, to assess the strength of your relationship credibility, ask yourself, Do those I am hoping to persuade see me as helpful, trustworthy, and supportive? Will they see is a process of give-and-take. Kathleen Reardon, a professor of organizational behavior at the University of Southern California, points out that a persuader rarely changes another person's behavior or viewpoint without altering his or her own in the process. To persuade meaningfully, we must not only listen to others but also incorporate their perspectives into our own.

3. **They think the secret of persuasion lies in presenting great arguments.** In persuading people to change their minds, great arguments matter. No doubt about it. But arguments, per se, are only one part of the equation. Other factors matter just as much, such as the persuader's credibility and his or her ability to create a proper, mutually beneficial frame for a position, connect on the right emotional level with an audience, and communicate through vivid language that makes arguments come alive.

4. **They assume persuasion is a one-shot effort.** Persuasion is a process, not an event. Rarely, if ever, is it possible to arrive at a shared solution on the first try. More often than not, persuasion involves listening to people, testing a position, developing a new position that reflects input from the group, more testing, incorporating compromises, and then trying again. If this sounds like a slow and difficult process, that's because it is. But the results are worth the effort.

---

me as someone in sync with them—emotionally, intellectually, and politically—on issues like this one? Finally, it is important to note that it is not enough to get your own read on these matters. You must also test your answers with colleagues you trust to give you a reality check. Only then will you have a complete picture of your credibility.

In most cases, that exercise helps people discover that they have some measure of weakness, either on the expertise or on the relationship side of credibility. The challenge then becomes to fill in such gaps.

In general, if your area of weakness is on the expertise side, you have several options:

- First, you can learn more about the complexities of your position through either formal or informal education and through conversations with knowledgeable individuals. You might also get more relevant experience on the job by asking, for instance, to be assigned to a team that would increase your insight into particular markets or products.

- Another alternative is to hire someone to bolster your expertise—for example, an industry consultant or a recognized outside expert, such as a professor. Either one may have the knowledge and experience required to support your position effectively. Similarly, you may tap experts within your organization to advocate your position. Their credibility becomes a substitute for your own.

- You can also utilize other outside sources of information to support your position, such as respected business or trade periodicals, books, independently produced reports, and lectures by experts. In our research, one executive from the clothing industry successfully persuaded his company to reposition an entire product line to a more youthful market after bolstering his credibility with articles by a noted demographer in two highly regarded journals and with two independent market-research studies.

- Finally, you may launch pilot projects to demonstrate on a small scale your expertise and the value of your ideas.

As for filling in the relationship gap:

- You should make a concerted effort to meet one-on-one with all the key people you plan to persuade. This is not the time to outline your position but rather to get a range of perspectives on the issue at hand. If you have the time and resources, you should even offer to help these people with issues that concern them.

- Another option is to involve like-minded coworkers who already have strong relationships with your audience. Again, that is a matter of seeking out substitutes on your own behalf.

For an example of how these strategies can be put to work, consider the case of a chief operating officer of a large retail bank, whom we will call Tom Smith. Although he was new to his job, Smith ardently wanted to persuade the senior management team that the company was in serious trouble. He believed that the bank's overhead was excessive and would jeopardize its position as the industry entered a more competitive era. Most of his colleagues, however, did not see the potential seriousness of the situation. Because the bank had been enormously successful in recent years, they believed changes in the industry posed little danger. In addition to being newly appointed, Smith had another problem: his career had been in financial services, and he was considered an outsider in the world of retail banking. Thus he had few personal connections to draw on as he made his case, nor was he perceived to be particularly knowledgeable about marketplace exigencies.

As a first step in establishing credibility, Smith hired an external consultant with respected credentials in the industry who showed that the bank was indeed poorly positioned to be a low-cost producer. In a series of interactive presentations to the bank's top-level management, the consultant revealed how the company's leading competitors were taking aggressive actions to contain operating costs. He made it clear from these presentations that not cutting costs would soon cause the bank to fall drastically behind the competition. These findings were then distributed in written reports that circulated throughout the bank.

Next, Smith determined that the bank's branch managers were critical to his campaign. The buy-in of those respected and informed individuals would signal to others in the company that his concerns were valid. Moreover, Smith looked to the branch managers because he believed that they could increase his expertise about marketplace trends and also help him test his own assumptions. Thus, for the next three months, he visited every branch in his region of Ontario, Canada—135 in all. During each visit, he spent time with branch managers, listening to their perceptions of the bank's strengths and weaknesses. He learned firsthand about the competition's initiatives and customer trends, and he solicited ideas for improving the bank's services and minimizing costs. By the time he was through, Smith had a broad perspective on the bank's future that few people even in senior management possessed. And he had built dozens of relationships in the process.

Finally, Smith launched some small but highly visible initiatives to demonstrate his expertise and capabilities. For example, he was concerned about slow growth in the company's mortgage business and the loan officers' resulting slip in morale. So he devised a program in which new mortgage customers would make no payments for the first 90 days. The initiative proved remarkably successful, and in short order Smith appeared to be a far more savvy retail banker than anyone had assumed.

Another example of how to establish credibility comes from Microsoft. In 1990, two product-development managers, Karen Fries and Barry Linnett, came to believe that the market would greatly welcome software that featured a "social interface." They envisioned a package that would employ animated human and animal characters to show users how to go about their computing tasks.

Inside Microsoft, however, employees had immediate concerns about the concept. Software programmers ridiculed the cute characters. Animated characters had been used before only in software for children, making their use in adult environments hard to envision. But Fries and Linnett felt their proposed product had both dynamism and complexity, and they remained convinced that consumers would eagerly buy such programs. They also believed that the home-computer software market—largely untapped at the time and with fewer software standards—would be open to such innovation.

Within the company, Fries had gained quite a bit of relationship credibility. She had started out as a recruiter for the company in 1987 and had worked directly for many of Microsoft's senior executives. They trusted and liked her. In addition, she had been responsible for hiring the company's product and program managers. As a result, she knew all the senior people at Microsoft and had hired many of the people who would be deciding on her product.

Linnett's strength laid in his expertise. In particular, he knew the technology behind an innovative tutorial program called PC Works.

In addition, both Fries and Linnett had managed Publisher, a product with a unique help feature called Wizards, which Microsoft's CEO, Bill Gates, had liked. But those factors were sufficient only to get an initial hearing from Microsoft's senior management. To persuade the organization to move forward, the pair would need to improve perceptions of their expertise. It hurt them that this type of social-interface software had no proven track record of success and that they were both novices with such software. Their challenge became one of finding substitutes for their own expertise.

Their first step was a wise one. From within Microsoft, they hired respected technical guru Darrin Massena. With Massena, they developed a set of prototypes to demonstrate that they did indeed understand the software's technology and could make it work. They then tested the prototypes in market research, and users responded enthusiastically. Finally, and most important, they enlisted two Stanford University professors, Clifford Nass and Bryon Reeves, both experts in human-computer interaction. In several meetings with Microsoft senior managers and Gates himself, they presented a rigorously compiled and thorough body of research that demonstrated how and why social-interface software was ideally suited to the average computer user. In addition, Fries and Linnett asserted that considerable jumps in computing power would make more realistic cartoon characters an increasingly malleable technology. Their product, they said, was the leading edge of an incipient software revolution. Convinced, Gates approved a full product-development team, and in January 1995, the product called BOB was launched. BOB went on to sell more than half a million copies, and its concept and technology are being used within Microsoft as a platform for developing several Internet products.

Credibility is the cornerstone of effective persuading; without it, a persuader won't be given the time of day. In the best-case scenario, people enter into a persuasion situation with some measure of expertise and relationship credibility. But it is important to note that credibility along either lines can be built or bought. Indeed, it must be, or the next steps are an exercise in futility.

Frame for common ground

Even if your credibility is high, your position must still appeal strongly to the people you are trying to persuade. After all, few people will jump on board a train that will bring them to ruin or even mild discomfort. Effective persuaders must be adept at describing their positions in terms that illuminate their advantages. As any parent can tell you, the fastest way to get a child to come along willingly on a trip to the grocery store is to point out that there are lollipops by the cash register. That is not deception. It is just a persuasive way of framing the benefits of taking such a journey. In work situations, persuasive framing is obviously more complex, but the underlying principle is the same. It is a process of identifying shared benefits.

Monica Ruffo, an account executive for an advertising agency, offers a good example of persuasive framing. Her client, a fast-food chain, was instituting a promotional campaign in Canada; menu items such as a hamburger, fries, and cola were to be bundled together and sold at a low price. The strategy made sense to corporate headquarters. Its research showed that consumers thought the company's products were higher priced than the competition's, and the company was anxious to overcome this perception. The franchisees, on the other hand, were still experiencing strong sales and were far more concerned about the short-term impact that the new, low prices would have on their profit margins.

A less experienced persuader would have attempted to rationalize headquarters' perspective to the franchisees—to convince them of its validity. But Ruffo framed the change in pricing to demonstrate its benefits to the franchisees themselves. The new value campaign, she explained, would actually improve franchisees' profits. To back up this point, she drew on several sources. A pilot project in Tennessee, for instance, had demonstrated that under the new pricing scheme, the sales of french fries and drinks—the two most profitable items on the menu—had markedly increased. In addition, the company had rolled out medium-sized meal packages in 80% of its U.S. outlets, and franchisees' sales of fries and drinks had jumped 26%. Citing research from a respected business periodical, Ruffo also showed that when customers raised their estimate of the value they receive from a retail establishment by 10%, the establishment's sales rose by 1%. She had estimated that the new meal plan would increase value perceptions by 100%, with the result that franchisee sales could be expected to grow 10%.

Ruffo closed her presentation with a letter written many years before by the company's founder to the organization. It was an emotional letter extolling the values of the company and stressing the importance of the franchisees to the company's success. It also highlighted the importance of the company's position as the low-price leader in the industry. The beliefs and values contained in the letter had long been etched in the minds of Ruffo's audience. Hearing them again only confirmed the company's concern for the franchisees and the importance of their winning formula. They also won Ruffo a standing ovation. That day, the franchisees voted unanimously to support the new meal-pricing plan.

The Ruffo case illustrates why—in choosing appropriate positioning—it is critical first to identify your objective's tangible benefits to the people you are trying to persuade. Sometimes that is easy. Mutual benefits exist. In other situations, however, no shared advantages are readily apparent—or meaningful. In these cases, effective persuaders adjust their positions. They know it is impossible to engage people and gain commitment to ideas or plans without highlighting the advantages to all the parties involved.

At the heart of framing is a solid understanding of your audience. Even before starting to persuade, the best persuaders we have encountered closely study the issues that matter to their colleagues. They use conversations, meetings, and other forms of dialogue to collect essential information. They are good at listening. They test their ideas with trusted confidants, and they ask questions of the people they will later be persuading. Those steps help them think through the arguments, the evidence, and the perspectives they will present. Oftentimes, this process causes them to alter or compromise their own plans before they even start persuading. It is through this thoughtful, inquisitive approach they develop frames that appeal to their audience.

Consider the case of a manager who was in charge of process engineering for a jet engine manufacturer. He had redesigned the work flow for routine turbine maintenance for airline clients in a manner that would dramatically shorten the turnaround time for servicing. Before presenting his ideas to the company's president, he consulted a good friend in the company, the vice president of engineering, who knew the president well. This conversation revealed that the president's prime concern would not be speed or efficiency but profitability. To get the president's buy-in, the vice president explained, the new system would have to improve the company's profitability in the short run by lowering operating expenses.

At first this information had the manager stumped. He had planned to focus on efficiency and had even intended to request additional funding to make the process work. But his conversation with the vice president sparked him to change his position. Indeed, he went so far as to change the work-flow design itself so that it no longer required new investment but rather drove down costs. He then carefully documented the cost savings and profitability gains that his new plan would produce and presented this revised plan to the president. With his initiative positioned anew, the manager persuaded the president and got the project approved.

Provide evidence

With credibility established and a common frame identified, persuasion becomes a matter of presenting evidence. Ordinary evidence, however, won't do. We have found that the most effective persuaders use language in a particular way. They supplement numerical data with examples, stories, metaphors, and analogies to make their positions come alive. That use of language paints a vivid word picture and, in doing so, lends a compelling and tangible quality to the persuader's point of view.

Think about a typical persuasion situation. The persuader is often advocating a goal, strategy, or initiative with an uncertain outcome. Karen Fries and Barry Linnett, for instance, wanted Microsoft to invest millions of dollars in a software package with chancy technology and unknown market demand. The team could have supported its case solely with market research, financial projections, and the like. But that would have been a mistake, because research shows that most people perceive such reports as not entirely informative. They are too abstract to be completely meaningful or memorable. In essence, the numbers don't make an emotional impact.

By contrast, stories and vivid language do, particularly when they present comparable situations to the one under discussion. A marketing manager trying to persuade senior executives to invest in a new product, for example, might cite examples of similar investments that paid off handsomely. Indeed, we found that people readily draw lessons from such cases. More important, the research shows that listeners absorb information in proportion to its vividness. Thus it is no wonder that Fries and Linnett hit a home run when they presented their case for BOB with the following analogy:

Imagine you want to cook dinner and you must first go to the supermarket. You have all the flexibility you want—you can cook anything in the world as long as you know how and have the time and desire to do it. When you arrive at the supermarket, you find all these overstuffed aisles with cryptic single-word headings like "sundries" and "ethnic food" and "condiments." These are the menus on typical computer interfaces. The question is whether salt is under condiments or ethnic food or near the potato chip section. There are surrounding racks and wall spaces, much as our software interfaces now have support buttons, tool bars, and lines around the perimeters. Now after you have collected everything, you still need to put it all together in the correct order to make a meal. If you're a good cook, your meal will probably be good. If you're a novice, it probably won't be.

We [at Microsoft] have been selling under the supermarket category for years, and we think there is a big opportunity for restaurants. That's what we are trying to do now with BOB: pushing the next step with software that is more like going to a restaurant, so the user doesn't spend all of his time searching for the ingredients. We find and put the ingredients together. You sit down, you get comfortable. We bring you a menu. We do the work, you relax. It's an enjoyable experience. No walking around lost trying to find things, no cooking.

Had Fries and Linnett used a literal description of BOB's advantages, few of their highly computer-literate colleagues at Microsoft would have personally related to the menu-searching frustration that BOB was designed to eliminate. The analogy they selected, however, made BOB's purpose both concrete and memorable.

A master persuader, Mary Kay Ash, the founder of Mary Kay Cosmetics, regularly draws on analogies to illustrate and "sell" the business conduct she values. Consider this speech at the company's annual sales convention:

> Back in the days of the Roman Empire, the legions of the emperor conquered the known world. There was, however, one band of people that the Romans never conquered. Those people were the followers of the great teacher from Bethlehem. Historians have long since discovered that one of the reasons for the sturdiness of this folk was their habit of meeting together weekly. They shared their difficulties, and they stood side by side. Does this remind you of something? The way we stand side by side and share our knowledge and difficulties with each other in our weekly unit meetings? I have so often observed when a director or unit member is confronted with a personal problem that the unit stands together in helping that sister in distress. What a wonderful circle of friendships we have. Perhaps it's one of the greatest fringe benefits of our company.

Through her vivid analogy, Ash links collective support in the company to a courageous period in Christian history. In doing so, she accomplishes several objectives. First, she drives home her belief that collective support is crucial to the success of the organization. Most Mary Kay salespeople are independent operators who face the daily challenges of direct selling. An emotional support system of fellow salespeople is essential to ensure that self-esteem and confidence remain intact in the face of rejection. Next she suggests by her analogy that solidarity against the odds is the best way to stymie powerful oppressors—to wit, the competition. Finally, Ash's choice of analogy imbues a sense of a heroic mission to the work of her sales force.

You probably don't need to invoke the analogy of the Christian struggle to support your position, but effective persuaders are not afraid of unleashing the immense power of language. In fact, they use it to their utmost advantage.

Connect emotionally

In the business world, we like to think that our colleagues use reason to make their decisions, yet if we scratch below the surface we will always find emotions at play. Good persuaders are aware of the primacy of emotions and are responsive to them in two important ways. First, they show their own emotional commitment to the position they are advocating. Such expression is a delicate matter. If you act too emotional, people may doubt your clearheadedness. But you must also show that your commitment to a goal is not just in your mind but in your heart and gut as well. Without this demonstration of feeling, people may wonder if you actually believe in the position you're championing.

Perhaps more important, however, is that effective persuaders have a strong and accurate sense of their audience's emotional state, and they adjust the tone of their arguments accordingly. Sometimes that means coming on strong, with forceful points. Other times, a whisper may be all that is required. The idea is that whatever your position, you match your emotional fervor to your audience's ability to receive the message.

Effective persuaders seem to have a second sense about how their colleagues have interpreted past events in the organization and how they will probably interpret a proposal. The best persuaders in our study would usually canvass key individuals who had a good pulse on the mood and emotional expectations of those about to be persuaded. They would ask those individuals how various proposals might affect colleagues on an emotional level—in essence, testing possible reactions. They were also quite effective at gathering information through informal conversations in the hallways or at lunch. In the end, their aim was to ensure that the emotional appeal behind their persuasion matched what their audience was already feeling or expecting.

To illustrate the importance of emotional matchmaking in persuasion, consider this example. The president of an aeronautics manufacturing company strongly believed that the maintenance costs and turnaround time of the company's U.S. and foreign competitors were so much better than his own company's that it stood to lose customers and profits. He wanted to communicate his fear and his urgent desire for change to his senior managers. So one afternoon, he called them into the boardroom. On an overhead screen was the projected image of a smiling man flying an old-fashioned biplane with his scarf blowing in the wind. The right half of the transparency was covered. When everyone was seated, the president explained that he felt as this pilot did, given the company's recent good fortune. The organization, after all, had just finished its most successful year in history. But then with a deep sigh, he announced that his happiness was quickly vanishing. As the president lifted the remaining portion of the sheet, he revealed an image of the pilot flying directly into a wall. The president then faced his audience and in a heavy voice said, "This is what I see happening to us." He asserted that the company was headed for a crash if people didn't take action fast. He then went on to lecture the group about the steps needed to counter this threat.

The reaction from the group was immediate and negative. Directly after the meeting, managers gathered in small clusters in the hallways to talk about the president's "scare tactics." They resented what they perceived to be the president's overstatement of the case. As the managers saw it, they had exerted enormous effort that year to break the company's records in sales and profitability. They were proud of their achievements. In fact, they had entered the meeting expecting it would be the moment of recognition. But to their absolute surprise, they were scolded.

The president's mistake? First, he should have canvassed a few members of his senior team to ascertain the emotional state of the group. From that, he would have learned that they were in need of thanks and recognition. He should then have held a separate session devoted simply to praising the team's accomplishments. Later, in a second meeting, he could have expressed his own anxieties about the coming year. And rather than blame the team for ignoring the future, he could have calmly described what he saw as emerging threats to the company and then asked his management team to help him develop new initiatives.

Now let us look at someone who found the right emotional match with his audience: Robert Marcell, head of Chrysler's small-car design team. In the early 1990s, Chrysler was eager to produce a new subcompact—indeed, the company had not introduced a new model of this type since 1978. But senior managers at Chrysler did not want to go it alone. They thought an alliance with a foreign manufacturer would improve the car's design and protect Chrysler's cash stores.

Marcell was convinced otherwise. He believed that the company should bring the design and production of a new subcompact in-house. He knew that persuading senior managers would be difficult, but he also had his own team to contend with. Team members had lost their confidence that they would ever again have the opportunity to create a good car. They were also angry that the United States had once again given up its position to foreign competitors when it came to small cars.

Marcell decided that his persuasion tactics had to be built around emotional themes that would touch his audience. From innumerable conversations around the company, he learned that many people felt as he did—that to surrender the subcompact's design to a foreign manufacturer was to surrender the company's soul and, ultimately, its ability to provide jobs. In addition, he felt deeply that his organization was a talented group hungry for a challenge and an opportunity to restore its self-esteem and pride. He would need to demonstrate his faith in the team's abilities.

Marcell prepared a 15-minute talk built around slides of his hometown, Iron River, a now defunct mining town in Upper Michigan, devastated, in large part, by foreign mining companies. On the screen flashed recent photographs he had taken of his boarded-up high school, the shuttered homes of his childhood friends, the crumbling ruins of the town's ironworks, closed churches, and an abandoned railroad yard. After a description of each of these places, he said the phrase, "We couldn't compete"—like the refrain of a hymn. Marcell's point was that the same outcome awaited Detroit if the production of small cars was not brought back to the United States. Surrender was the enemy, he said, and devastation would follow if the group did not take immediate action.

Marcell ended his slide show on a hopeful note. He spoke of his pride in his design group and then challenged the team to build a "made-in-America" subcompact that would prove that the United States could still compete. The speech, which echoed the exact sentiments of the audience, rekindled the group's fighting spirit. Shortly after the speech, group members began drafting their ideas for a new car.

Marcell then took his slide show to the company's senior management and ultimately to Chrysler chairman Lee Iacocca. As Marcell showed his slides, he could see that Iacocca was touched. Iacocca, after all, was a fighter and a strongly patriotic man himself. In fact, Marcell's approach was not too different from Iacocca's earlier appeal to the United States Congress to save Chrysler. At the end of the show, Marcell stopped and said, "If we dare to be different, we could be the reason the U.S. auto industry survives. We could be the reason our kids and grandkids don't end up working at fast-food chains." Iacocca stayed on for two hours as Marcell explained in greater detail what his team was planning. Afterward, Iacocca changed his mind and gave Marcell's group approval to develop a car, the Neon.

With both groups, Marcell skillfully matched his emotional tenor to that of the group he was addressing. The ideas he conveyed resonated deeply with his largely Midwestern audience. And rather than leave them in a depressed state, he offered them hope, which was more persuasive than promising doom. Again, this played to the strong patriotic sentiments of his American-heartland audience.

No effort to persuade can succeed without emotion, but showing too much emotion can be as unproductive as showing too little. The important point to remember is that you must match your emotions to your audience's.

The Force of Persuasion

The concept of persuasion, like that of power, often confuses and even mystifies businesspeople. It is so complex—and so dangerous when mishandled—that many would rather just avoid it altogether. But like power, persuasion can be a force for enormous good in an organization. It can pull people together, move ideas forward, galvanize change, and forge constructive solutions. To do all that, however, people must understand persuasion for what it is—not convincing and selling but learning and negotiating. Furthermore, it must be seen as an art form that requires commitment and practice, especially as today's business contingencies make persuasion more necessary than ever.

Originally published in May 1998. Reprint 98304

Is Silence Killing Your Company?

by Leslie Perlow and Stephanie Williams

SILENCE IS ASSOCIATED WITH MANY virtues: modesty, respect for others, prudence, decorum. Thanks to deeply ingrained rules of etiquette, people silence themselves to avoid embarrassment, confrontation, and other perceived dangers. There's an old saying that sums up the virtues of silence: "Better to be quiet and thought a fool than to talk and be known as one."

The social virtues of silence are reinforced by our survival instincts. Many organizations send the message—verbally or nonverbally—that falling into line is the safest way to hold on to our jobs and further our careers. The need for quiet submission is exaggerated by today's difficult economy, where millions of people have lost their jobs and many more worry that they might. A Dilbert cartoon poignantly expresses how pointless—and perilous—many people feel it is to speak out. Dilbert, the everyman underling, recognizes that a senior executive is making a poor decision. "Shouldn't we tell her?" he asks his boss, who laughs cynically. "Yes," the boss replies. "Let's end our careers by challenging a decision that won't change. That's a great idea."

To be sure, people who speak out sometimes get their day in the sun: Sherron Watkins of Enron, Cynthia Cooper of WorldCom, and Coleen Rowley at the FBI all ended up on the cover of *Time* as "Persons of the Year." But public recognition of a few people does not mean that speaking out is necessarily viewed as courageous or praiseworthy.

Most individuals who go against their organizations or express their concerns publicly are severely punished. If they're not fired outright, they're usually marginalized and made to feel irrelevant.

But it is time to take the gilt off silence. Our research shows that silence is not only ubiquitous and expected in organizations but extremely costly to both the firm and the individual. Our interviews with senior executives and employees in organizations ranging from small businesses to *Fortune* 500 corporations to government bureaucracies reveal that silence can exact a high psychological price on individuals, generating feelings of humiliation, pernicious anger, resentment, and the like that, if unexpressed, contaminate every interaction, shut down creativity, and undermine productivity.

Take the case of Jeff, a team leader at a *Fortune* 100 company who was working on a large, long-term, high-pressure project. Each Tuesday, Jeff and his peers had a project management meeting (PMM) with Matt, their boss. Jeff would start writing his weekly update reports on Wednesday, continuing to work on them when he had time on Thursday and Friday, working even into the weekend. On Monday morning, he would hand in his document to Matt. Jeff figured that a weekly update was probably useful for Matt; all the same, he felt deeply frustrated at the time he was wasting writing the elaborate reports. Yet despite complaining endlessly to his peers, week after week Jeff said nothing to Matt. With each act of silence, Jeff's resentment grew and his respect for Matt disintegrated, even as Jeff became more and more uncomfortable with the idea of questioning Matt. And so the process continued, as the project fell further behind schedule. For his part, when Matt was asked about the value of the PMM, he was mystified: "Not to insult my team leaders, but in my mind, every Tuesday morning I have a Painfully Meaningless Meeting."

The fact that no one suggested an alternative to the PMM was fairly typical of our findings. Individuals are frequently convinced that keeping quiet is the best way to preserve relationships and get work done. In the following pages, we will examine what makes this sort of silence so prevalent in organizations. From there, we will discuss the personal and organizational costs of silence, which often

Idea in Brief

Many times, often with the best of intentions, people at work decide it's more productive to remain silent about their differences than to air them. There's no time, they think, or no point in going against what the boss says.

But as new research by the authors shows, silencing doesn't smooth things over or make people more productive. It merely pushes differences beneath the surface and can set in motion powerfully destructive forces. When people stay silent about important disagreements, they can begin to fill with anxiety, anger, and resentment. As long as the conflict is unresolved, their repressed feelings remain potent, making them increasingly distrustful, self-protective, and all the more fearful that if they speak up they will be embarrassed or rejected. Their sense of insecurity grows, leading to further acts of silence, more defensiveness, and more distrust, thereby setting into

motion a destructive "spiral of silence." Sooner or later, they mentally opt out—sometimes merely doing what they're told but contributing nothing of their own, sometimes spreading discontent and frustration throughout the workplace that can lead them, and others, to leave without thinking it through.

These vicious spirals of silence can be replaced with virtuous spirals of communication, but that requires individuals to find the courage to act differently and executives to create the conditions in which people will value the expression of differences. All too often, behind failed products, broken processes, and mistaken career decisions are people who chose to hold their tongues. Breaking the silence can bring an outpouring of fresh ideas from all levels of an organization—ideas that might just raise the organization's performance to a whole new level.

remain hidden for long periods of time even as they grow exponentially with each additional act of silence. Finally, we will investigate several ways to break free from the insidious silent sink.

The Reign of Silence

Silence often starts when we choose not to confront a difference. Given the dissimilarities in our temperaments, backgrounds, and experiences, it's inevitable that we will have different opinions, beliefs, and tastes. Most of us recognize the value of such variety: Who really wants to go into a brainstorming session with people who all have the same views and ideas? But we're also aware of how terribly painful it can be to raise and work through differences. The French word *différend,* tellingly, means "quarrel." Not surprisingly, most people decide it's easier to cover up their differences than to try to discuss them.

Our research shows that this tendency to remain silent rather than express a difference exists both in individual relationships and in groups, where we fear a loss of status or even expulsion if we differ from the rest. Most of us can remember from our adolescence how compelling the desire was to conform. Even as adults, many people in organizations are willing to go to enormous lengths to get along with members of their work groups—at least superficially. We do what we believe other group members want us to do. We say what we think other people want us to say.

Consider what happened at one off-site meeting of top management at a Web-based education company. Concerned about the company's vision, the managers met to share and discuss different perspectives. But one speaker after another just echoed what the previous speaker had said. When any manager did dare to dissent, a colleague would quickly dismiss his idea. Having effectively tabled every discussion in which disagreement surfaced, the management team crowed about the level of "consensus" they had achieved. One by one, team members celebrated their achievement. The head of marketing went first. "We made some great progress today," he said, "I'm excited—passionate—committed to the future." The CFO continued, "I thought today was going to be a lot uglier. I expected battles. Yet things were remarkably consistent." Yet despite the outward expression of consensus, at the end of the day, many of the attendees privately despaired that the off-site had been a waste of time. By silencing themselves and one another, they failed to create a compelling vision, and the company continued with no clear direction.

This meeting shows how the pressure for unanimity can prevent employees of roughly equal grade and status—even top managers—from exploring their differences. More familiar to many is the pressure to keep silent that's created by differences in rank. How easy it is for a boss to send a powerful signal that a worker should be quiet. Take the case of Robert and Linda. Robert was an attorney in charge of his law firm's support staff. Linda, who was head of the library, came to Robert one day to complain about the performance evaluation process. She felt that many of the lawyers weren't being fair in their evaluations of the library staff and that they shouldn't have the automatic right to determine the librarians' raises and promotions. Robert disagreed. "If you think of the lawyers as your clients," he advised, "you can see why they have every expectation to be able to critique the quality of service." When Linda pressed again, Robert got irritated and said, "This is the way we do it around here, and this is the way it's going to continue!" Linda said nothing more and quietly left his office.

At least Linda tried to speak up. Many members of organizations silence themselves before the boss has the slightest inkling of what they're thinking. Often in these instances, employees use silence as a strategy to get ahead. Consider Don, a senior analyst at an investment bank who carefully keeps his opinions to himself when he's around his superiors. "It comes down to the hierarchical nature of the bank," he says. "Basically you're just trying to make the person above you love you so you'll get a big bonus. If you start raising uncomfortable questions and being holier-than-thou, you may be absolutely right, but you shoot yourself in the foot. What the managing director says goes."

And it's not just that subordinates feel pressure to keep silent with their bosses. Bosses also may feel uncomfortable expressing their differences with subordinates. It is frequently difficult for managers, for instance, to give negative performance feedback to subordinates—especially in organizations that place a high value on being polite and avoiding confrontation.

The Costs of Suffering in Silence

When we silence ourselves and others—even when we're convinced that it is the best way, the right way, or the only way to preserve the relationships we care about and get on with our work—we may be

When to Zip It

ALTHOUGH MOST PEOPLE TEND TO speak up too little rather than too much, there are times when it's better to stay quiet. Some issues are simply not worth raising, and you don't want to unnecessarily turn small differences of opinion into broad conflicts. There's no sense in spending time and effort getting bogged down dealing with every little difference, especially ones that are not likely to affect the quality of people's work or those you're not likely to remember in a week or a month. And if the conflict is in an unimportant relationship or one that won't continue much longer, speaking up may not be crucial. You will still lose out on the creativity and learning that stem from expressing differences, but you don't need to worry about the additional costs of unresolved differences lurking beneath the surface and destroying the relationship.

Even when a difference should be addressed, there is the question of timing. It may be fruitless, for example, to raise a tough issue with your boss when you face an impending deadline—unless speaking up is important for the task at hand and there really is enough time to work through the issue. Waiting until the deadline has passed and people can focus on what you have to say may be the best option. Moreover, initially keeping a lid on differences when your own or the other person's emotions are highly charged can be beneficial in the longer run. If you've just had a row with a colleague and either of you is very upset, arrange a time to talk in the future when both of you have had a chance to cool down and can discuss differences without venting or blaming. But if you defer a difficult conversation, make sure you do not postpone it indefinitely. Otherwise, the unresolved differences will come back to haunt you.

There are no hard-and-fast rules about what needs to be discussed or when it's best to do so. You must rely on your best judgment. What's important is that you shift your mind-set from asking whether this is one of those rare times when you should speak to asking instead whether this is one of those rare times when you should remain quiet.

---

fooling ourselves. Let's return for a moment to the law firm where Robert and Linda worked. After meeting with Linda, Robert simply forgot about their discussion. As a senior partner, he thought his view was a no-brainer, and he assumed that the issue would just go away. Linda, for her part, was acutely aware that she had been forced into silence, but, given that Robert was the boss, she thought the best course was to say nothing further to him.

Still, she was profoundly angry. In an attempt to release her negative feelings, she complained bitterly to her peers about what Robert
had said and how he had shut her down. But gossiping only allevi-
ated Linda's anger temporarily, and news of Robert's insensitivity
quickly spread throughout the support staff, which came to view the
incident as evidence that "management doesn't listen." Ultimately,
Robert's strained relations with the support staff led to high
turnover. As he later reflected, "My action that day was probably the
single greatest mistake I ever made."

The damage wasn't just to Robert and the organization. Linda, in
choosing to respond to Robert with silence, caused herself great
damage as well, far more in fact than she may have realized. That's
because silencing doesn't resolve anything; rather than erase differences, it merely pushes them beneath the surface. Every time we
keep silent about our differences, we swell with negative emotions
like anxiety, anger, and resentment. Of course, we can go on for a
long time pretending to ourselves and others that nothing is wrong.
But as long as the conflict is not resolved, our repressed feelings remain potent and color the way we relate to other people. We begin to
feel a sense of disconnection in our relationships, which in turn
causes us to become increasingly self-protective.

When we feel defensive in this way, we become all the more
fearful that if we speak up we will be embarrassed or rejected. Our
sense of insecurity grows. In relationships we care about preserv-
ing, more acts of silence follow, which only bring more defensiveness and more distrust. A destructive "spiral of silence" is set in
motion.

Caught up in just such a spiral was Maria, a project manager we
interviewed at a management consulting firm. At the beginning of
her first project, her boss, Max, suggested to Maria ways her team
should make its initial presentation to the client. Maria wasn't convinced that Max's approach was the best. But Max was the partner,
so Maria kept her concerns to herself. Later, when Max discovered
that the team had failed to collect some of the data he wanted, he
lost his temper and ordered Maria to push the team harder. Maria
thought that the data were irrelevant and that searching for them

Speed Trap

THERE'S NO DOUBT THAT PRESSURE to go fast can have its benefits. It can, for example, push us to find more efficient, less bureaucratic ways of working. But it also makes us even more likely to keep silent. How many times has a looming deadline caused you to bite your tongue and think to yourself, "We don't have time to worry about this now; we just need to get it done."

When we perpetually silence ourselves in the short-sighted belief that we are getting our tasks done as expeditiously as possible, we may interfere with creativity, learning, and decision making. If our work depends on divergent thinking, these less-effective processes may in turn result in problems that take time and attention to resolve. Then, in addition to all the work we are rushing to complete, we will also have to address these new problems. That can lead to a vicious cycle that makes us feel the need to go even faster. A little fable about a farmer with a wagon full of apples helps illustrate the point. The farmer stopped a man on the side of the road and asked how far it was to market. The man responded, "It is an hour away, if you go slow." He continued, "If you go fast, it will take you all day." There was a bump in the road, and if the farmer went too fast he would hit it, all his apples would fall out, and he'd

would just waste the team's time. But, inwardly clenching her fists and gritting her teeth, she deferred to her superior.

A few days later, Maria and her team received a lukewarm response when they presented their findings to the client. Maria later met with Max to discuss the next steps. Convinced that she understood the client's needs better than he did, she was intent on laying out her own point of view and explaining to him the error in his approach. But Maria had become very uncomfortable around Max, so when he launched into a critique of her team's performance, she lost her nerve. Again she stifled her resistance and opted to do as Max said. Maria's discomfort grew each time she chose to remain silent, and she descended down the spiral of silence. Ultimately, her desire and ability to work with Max were destroyed.

There's a cruel and all too common irony here, for the reason Maria had silenced herself in the first place was to preserve her relationship with Max. We don't speak up for fear of destroying our relationships, but in the end our silence creates an emotional distance that becomes an unbridgeable rift.

have to spend the day picking up the fruit. The farmer would then be in all the greater hurry to get to market.

The pressure to go fast ends up feeding on itself, perpetuating an internally generated and self-destructive, ever-increasing need for speed. Overstretched workers become more overstretched; managers already focused on crises become all the more so. In our daily lives, many of us face pressure to go fast, and we end up silencing our differences in response. We need to be careful, though, or we may end up in a self-made "speed trap."

In the end, whether our primary concern is to preserve our relationships or to get our tasks done as expeditiously as possible, we must speak up rather than withhold our differences. Otherwise, we risk undermining both our relationships and our ability to complete our work.[1]

1. For a more detailed discussion of how speed relates to silencing, see Leslie A. Perlow, Gerardo A. Okhuysen, and Nelson P. Repenning, "The Speed Trap: Exploring the Relationship Between Decision Making and the Temporal Context," *Academy of Management Journal* (October 2002).

That's what happened to Shoney, a research fellow in pulmonary and critical-care medicine. When we interviewed him, he had already discovered where the spiral leads. Praveen, a research associate one level higher, was supposed to oversee Shoney's work. In exchange, Praveen's name would appear on everything Shoney published. Eager to maximize Shoney's productivity, Praveen constantly issued him instructions. Shoney resented being bossed around but always did as he was told, never pushing back. Over time, however, Shoney's resentment grew as Praveen continued to treat him more like an unknowing assistant than a highly qualified peer. One day, when Praveen started to question Shoney about how he had spent his time in the lab the previous evening, something inside Shoney snapped. He still said nothing. But from that day forth, Shoney refused to collaborate with Praveen. On their next assignment, they divided the tasks and carried them out independently.

That just made things worse. By shutting himself off, Shoney lost the opportunity to brainstorm with an informed colleague. He also precluded the possibility of sharing anything he may have learned that could have helped Praveen. And he foreclosed on any potential for eliminating redundancy in the two researchers' work. Silencing was not only costly to Shoney, but it was a cost doubly borne, for the organization paid it as well. Each time workers remain silent in the face of conflict, they keep new ideas to themselves and leave alternative courses of action unexplored. And they withhold important information from colleagues that could enhance the quality of both their own and the organization's work.

Breaking the Spiral of Silence

How do we get ourselves and others to speak up? Can the vicious spirals of silence be replaced with virtuous spirals of communication? The answer is yes, but doing so requires that we find the courage to act differently and that we create the context in which people will value the expression of such difference. Managers with a lot of authority need to be especially careful not to punish people, explicitly or implicitly, for speaking out, particularly on issues that may be difficult for the organization to deal with. Harry's case illustrates how a leader can create such a context.

Harry was a battalion commander, whose unit of more than 500 soldiers had just been miserably defeated in a mock battle against another unit. "If this had been a real battle, two-thirds of us would be dead," Harry said to the unit in the debriefing that followed. But he continued, "I was at fault. I failed you." And he went on to explain exactly how, taking full responsibility for the failure.

At first, no one said a word. Then Nick, a very junior scout who was responsible for detecting and alerting the battalion to the enemy's movements, said, "No sir, it wasn't your fault. I fell asleep on duty."

Harry was shocked. But rather than focus on Nick's failure, great as it was, Harry immediately redirected the unit's attention to uncovering the underlying problem—the exhaustion his men were suffering. How many had also slept through the opening rounds of the attack, he asked his soldiers to think to themselves. "Nick is a good soldier," he said. "All of you are good soldiers. We need to focus on the bigger issue: How can we sustain our capabilities during continuous operations in such high-intensity situations?"

Harry set the tone for this discussion. Had he not started by exhibiting his own failures, it's highly unlikely that Nick would have had the courage to speak up. Moreover, Harry carefully framed the ensuing discussion to avoid blame and instead focus on the larger problem they all faced. In the end, this unit gained a rich appreciation for the importance of speaking up and admitting mistakes.

Keeping quiet is too big a problem to be left just to leaders, however. If an organization wants to escape the spiral of silence, everyone has to fight the urge to withdraw and has to work hard to speak up. That's a tough challenge, for all the reasons we've explored, but the following practices can help.

Recognize your power

We all have the power to express ourselves and to encourage others to speak freely, whether they're subordinates, peers, or even bosses. Of course, nobody likes to be the one to break the ice; in the face of personal conflict, passivity always feels safer than action. Who would not prefer to sit back, blame the other person, and wait for him to make the first move? Yet it's almost never the case that something is entirely another person's fault. Instead of waiting for the other person to apologize or to broach the subject, we need to be willing to take the first step ourselves—to bring differences out into the open so that they can be explored.

This can even be a good strategy for dealing with a boss who has overtly silenced a subordinate, like Robert, from the law firm. In that situation, Linda could have chosen to go back to Robert to try to turn the situation around. She could have met with him again and said something like, "I know that you don't think the issue with the performance evaluation process is important. But it is very important to the library staff, and we would like you to understand our point of view. I don't feel comfortable dropping the issue, as you suggested. I would like a chance to better explain my perspective."

When one person finds the courage to take a step like this and presents new information in a way that the other person can absorb, the two are likely to join in a process of mutual exploration of the differences that separate them. Indeed, we all have much more power than we think. Our superiors certainly have formal power over us, but it's also true that their performance depends on how well we are doing. Don't forget: Your boss needs you, too. And knowing that should empower you to speak up and help him appreciate your point of view.

Act deviantly

To break the walls of silence, sometimes we have to behave in ways that are not considered appropriate for our particular organization. Put differently, we must act deviantly—for example, by choosing to ask tough questions at a company meeting where employees normally just accept the decisions of top management. Although deviance often carries negative connotations, it is not synonymous with dysfunctionality. Deviance is, at heart, a creative act—a way of searching out and inventing new approaches to doing things. Acts of deviance can point to areas where organizations need to change and can result in fruitful alternatives. The chief thing to keep in mind here is that norms can have exceptions. By challenging a particular norm, we can play a role in changing it.

Build a coalition

Reaching out to others can give us the strength to break the hold of silence. Not only is it easier to speak up when we know we're not alone, but a coalition also carries more legitimacy and resources. Even though it may feel threatening to approach people to join forces with you, it is surprising how often you may find that many people feel the same way you do. That's what happened to Nancy Hopkins, a scientist at MIT.[1] Hopkins repeatedly found herself having to fight harder than her male colleagues for resources like lab space. After dealing with the same issues for years, she drafted a letter to the MIT administration. Before sending it, however, she showed it to a female colleague whom she regarded as politically savvy. To Hopkins's surprise, the other woman wanted to add her signature to the letter; the same type of things had happened to her, too. In the end, 14 of the 15 women Hopkins approached decided to sign as well. As a result, a committee was formed, and a pattern of discrimination was uncovered and addressed.

We've recently seen in the scandals at Enron, Tyco, and World-Com, to name but a few, just how catastrophic situations can become when silence prevails. Yet silence does not have to be about fraud and malfeasance to do grave damage to a company. All too often, behind failed products, broken processes, and mistaken decisions are people who chose to hold their tongues rather than to speak up. Breaking the silence can bring an outpouring of fresh ideas from all levels of an organization—ideas that might just raise the organization's performance to a whole new level.

Originally published in May 2003. Reprint R0305C

Note

1. The account here is taken from material in both Nancy H. Hopkins, "Experience of Women at the Massachusetts Institute of Technology," *Women in the Chemical Workforce: A Workshop Report to the Chemical Sciences Roundtable* (CPSMA, 2000) and Lotte Bailyn, "Academic Careers and Gender Equity: Lessons Learned from MIT," *Gender, Work, and Organizations* (March 2003).

How to Become an Authentic Speaker

by Nick Morgan

AT A COMPANYWIDE SALES MEETING, Carol, a vice president of sales, strides energetically to the podium, pauses for a few seconds to look at the audience, and then tells a story from her days as a field rep. She deftly segues from her anecdote to a positive assessment of the company's sales outlook for the year, supplementing her speech with colorful slides showing strong growth and exciting new products in the pipeline. While describing those products, she accents her words with animated gestures.

Having rehearsed carefully in front of a small audience of trusted colleagues, all of whom liked her message and her energy, she now confidently delivers the closer: Walking to the edge of the stage, she scans the room and challenges her listeners to commit to a stretch sales goal that will put many of them in the annual winners' circle.

But Carol senses that something's amiss. The audience isn't exhibiting the kind of enthusiasm needed to get the year off to a great start. She begins to panic: What's happening? Is there anything she can do to salvage the situation?

We all know a Carol. (You may be one yourself.) We've all heard speeches like hers, presentations in which the speaker is apparently doing all the right things, yet something—something we can't quite identify—is wrong.

If asked about these speeches, we might describe them as "calculated," "insincere," "not real," or "phoned in." We probably wouldn't be able to say exactly why the performance wasn't compelling. The speaker just didn't seem *authentic*.

In today's difficult economy, and especially in the aftermath of numerous scandals involving individual executives, employees and shareholders are more skeptical than ever. Authenticity—including the ability to communicate authentically with others—has become an important leadership attribute. When leaders have it, they can inspire their followers to make extraordinary efforts on behalf of their organizations. When they don't, cynicism prevails and few employees do more than the minimum necessary to get by.

In my 22 years of working as a communications coach, I have seen again and again how hard it is for managers to come across in public communications as authentic—even when they passionately believe their message. Why is this kind of communication so difficult? Why can't people just stand up and tell the truth?

What Science Teaches Us

The answer lies in recent research into the ways our brains perceive and process communication. We all know by now the power of nonverbal communication—what I call the "second conversation." If your spoken message and your body language are mismatched, audiences will respond to the nonverbal message every time. Gestures speak louder than words. And that means you *can't* just stand up and tell the truth. You'll often hear someone say in advance of a speech, "I don't want to look over-rehearsed, so I'm going to wing it." But during the presentation his body language will undermine his credibility. Because he's in a stressful situation with no preparation, he'll appear off-kilter. Whatever the message of his words, he'll seem to be learning as he goes—not likely to engender confidence in a leader.

So preparation is important. But the traditional approach—careful rehearsal like Carol's—often doesn't work either. That's because it usually involves specific coaching on nonverbal elements—"maintain eye

Idea in Brief

You rehearsed your speech thoroughly—and mastered that all-important body language. But when you delivered the talk, you sensed little enthusiasm in your audience.

What's going on? You're probably coming across as artificial. The reason: When we rehearse specific body language elements, we use them incorrectly during the actual speech—slightly *after* speaking the associated words. Listeners feel something's wrong, because during natural conversation, body language emerges *before* the associated words.

To demonstrate your authenticity, don't rehearse your body language. Instead, imagine meeting four aims:

- Being open to your audience
- Connecting with your audience
- Being passionate about your topic
- Listening to your audience

When you rehearse this way, you'll genuinely experience these feelings when delivering your speech. Your body language will emerge at the right moment. And your listeners will know you're the real thing.

contact," "spread your arms," "walk out from behind the podium"—that can ultimately make the speaker seem artificial. The audience can see the wheels turning in her head as she goes through the motions.

Why does this calculated body language come off as inauthentic? Here's where the brain research comes in. We're learning that in human beings the second, nonverbal conversation actually starts *first,* in the instant after an emotion or an impulse fires deep within the brain but before it has been articulated. Indeed, research shows that people's natural and unstudied gestures are often indicators of what they will think and say next.

You might say that words are after-the-fact explanations of why we just gestured as we did. Think of something as simple as a hug: The impulse to embrace someone begins *before* the thought that you're glad to see him or her has fully formed, much less been expressed aloud. Or think about a typical conversation: Reinforcement, contradiction, and commentary arise first in gesture. We nod vigorously, shake our heads, roll our eyes, all of which express our reactions more immediately—and more powerfully—than words can.

Idea in Practice

Morgan recommends rehearsing your speeches with these four aims in mind.

Being Open to Your Audience

To rehearse being open, practice your speech by envisioning what it would be like to give your presentation to someone you're completely comfortable with. The person could be your spouse, a close friend, or your child. Notice especially what this feels like: This is the emotional state you want to be in when you deliver the speech.

This state leads to more natural body language, such as smiles and relaxed shoulders. And the behaviors in turn lead to more candid expression of your thoughts and feelings.

Connecting with Your Audience

As you practice your speech, think about wanting to engage with your listeners. Imagine that a young child you know well isn't heeding you. You want to capture—and keep—his attention however you can.

In such situations, you don't strategize; you simply do what feels natural and appropriate. For example, you increase the intensity or volume of your voice or move closer to your listener. During your actual speech, these behaviors will happen naturally and with the right timing.

If gesture precedes conscious thought and thought precedes words—even if by no more than a tiny fraction of a second—that changes our thinking about speech preparation. When coached in the traditional way, rehearsing specific gestures one by one, speakers end up employing those gestures at the same time that—or even slightly after—they speak the associated words. Although audiences are not consciously aware of this unnatural sequence, their innate ability to read body language leads them to feel that something's wrong—that the speaker is inauthentic.

"Rehearsing" Authenticity

So if neither casual spontaneity nor traditional rehearsal leads to compelling communication, how can you prepare for an important presentation? You have to tap into the basic impulses underlying your speech. These should include four powerful aims: to be open,

Being Passionate About Your Topic

While rehearsing, ask yourself what in your topic you feel deeply about: What's at stake? What results do you want your presentation to produce? Focus not on what you want to say but on why you're giving the speech and how you feel about it. Let the underlying emotion come out in every word you deliver during rehearsal. You'll infuse the actual speech with some of that passion and come across as more human and engaging.

"Listening" to Your Audience

To practice fulfilling this aim, think about what your listeners will likely be feeling when you step up to begin your presentation. Are they excited about the future? Worried about bad news? As you practice, imagine watching them closely, looking for signs of their response to you.

During your presentation, you'll be more prepared to identify the emotions your listeners are sending to you via nonverbal means. And you'll be able to respond to them appropriately; for example, by picking up the pace, varying your language, asking an impromptu question, or even eliminating or changing parts of your talk.

to connect, to be passionate, and to listen. Each of these aims informs nearly all successful presentations.

Rehearse your speech with them in mind. Try practicing it four ways, adopting the mind-set of each aim in turn, feeling it more than thinking about it. Forget about rehearsing specific gestures. If you are able to sincerely realize these feelings, your body language will take care of itself, emerging naturally and at the right moment. (The approach described here may also lead you to refine some of your verbal message, to make it accord with your nonverbal one.) When you actually deliver the speech, continue to focus on the four underlying aims.

Note the paradox here. This method is designed to achieve authenticity through the mastery of a calculated process. But authenticity arises from the four aims, or what I call "intents," that I have mentioned. If you can physically and emotionally embody all four, you'll achieve the perceived *and* real authenticity that creates a powerful bond with listeners.

What Underlies an Authentic Speech

Creating that bond isn't easy. Let me offer some advice for tapping into each of the four intents.

The intent to be open with your audience

This is the first and in some ways the most important thing to focus on in rehearsing a speech, because if you come across as closed, your listeners will perceive you as defensive—as if they somehow represent a threat. Not much chance for communication there.

How can you become more open? Try to imagine giving your presentation to someone with whom you're completely relaxed— your spouse, a close friend, your child. Notice what that mental picture looks like but particularly what it *feels* like. This is the state you need to be in if you are to have an authentic rapport with your audience.

If it's hard to create this mental image, try the real thing. Find a patient friend and push yourself to be open with him or her. Notice what that scene looks like and, again, how you feel. Don't overintellectualize: This is a bit like practicing a golf swing or a tennis serve. Although you might make tiny mental notes about what you're doing, they shouldn't get in the way of recognizing a feeling that you can try to replicate later.

Openness immediately feels risky to many people. I worked with a CEO who was passionate about his work, but his audiences didn't respond. He realized that he'd learned as a boy not to show emotion precisely about the things that meant the most to him. We had to replace this felt experience with one of talking to a close friend he was excited to see.

Let's go back to Carol (a composite of several clients). As she works on feeling more open in her presentations, her face begins to light up with a big smile when she speaks, and her shoulders relax. She realizes that without meaning to, she has come across as so serious that she has alienated her audiences.

A change in nonverbal behavior can affect the spoken message. Over and over, I've seen clients begin speaking more comfortably—

and more authentically—as the intent to be more open physically led to a more candid expression of their thoughts.

The intent to connect with your audience

Once you begin to feel open, and you've stored away the memory of what it looks and feels like, you're ready to practice the speech again, this time focusing on the audience. Think about wanting—*needing*—to engage your listeners. Imagine that a young child you know well isn't heeding you. You want to capture that child's attention however you can. You don't strategize—you simply do what feels natural and appropriate. You increase the intensity or volume of your voice or move closer.

You also want to *keep* your audience's attention. Don't let listeners slide away into their thoughts instead of following yours. Here, you might transform your young child into a teenager and imagine yearning to keep this easily distractible listener focused on your words.

If openness is the ante that lets you into the game, connection is what keeps the audience playing. Now that Carol is intent on being connected with her listeners, she realizes that she typically waits too long—in fact, until the very end of her speech—to make contact with them. She begins her next presentation by reaching out to audience members who have contributed significantly to the company's sales success, establishing a connection that continues throughout her speech.

The intent to be passionate about your topic

Ask yourself what it is that you feel deeply about. What's at stake? What results do you want your presentation to produce? Are you excited about the prospects of your company? Worried that they look bleak? Determined to improve them?

Focus not on what you want to say but on why you're giving the speech and how you feel about that. Let the underlying emotion come out (once you've identified it, you won't need to force it) in every word you deliver during this round of rehearsal. Then raise the stakes for yourself: Imagine that somebody in the audience has the power to take everything away from you unless you win him or her over with your passionate argument.

I worked with a senior partner at a consulting firm who was planning to talk to her colleagues about the things at the firm she valued and wanted to pass on to the next generation as she got ready to retire. Her speech, when she began practicing it, was a crystal-clear but dull commentary on the importance of commitment and hard work. As she began focusing on the emotion beneath the speech, she recalled how her mother, a dancer, had instilled in her the value of persisting no matter what the obstacles. She decided to acknowledge her mother in her talk. She said that her mother, then 92, had never let the pain and difficulties she had experienced during her career obscure her joy in performing. Although the speaker shed most of her tears during rehearsal, her passion transformed the talk into something memorable.

Somewhat more prosaically, Carol begins to think about what she's passionate about—her determination to beat a close competitor—and how that might inform her presentations. She realizes that this passion fuels her energy and excitement about her job. She infuses her next speech with some of that passion and immediately comes across as more human and engaging.

The intent to "listen" to your audience

Now begin thinking about what your listeners are likely to be feeling when you step up to begin your presentation. Are they excited about the future? Worried about bad sales news? Hopeful they can keep their jobs after the merger? As you practice, imagine yourself watching them very closely, looking for signs of their response to you.

Of course, your intent to discover the audience's emotional state will be most important during the actual presentation. Usually your listeners won't actually be talking to you, but they will be sending you nonverbal messages that you'll need to pick up and respond to.

This isn't as hard as it may sound. As a fellow member of the human race, you are as expert as your audience in reading body language—if you have an intent to do so. As you read the messages your listeners are sending with their bodies, you may want to pick up the pace, vary your language, even change or eliminate parts of your talk. If this leads you to involve the audience in a real dialogue—say, by asking an impromptu question—so much the better.

If time has been set aside for questions at the end of your presentation, you'll want to listen to the audience with your whole body, keeping yourself physically and psychologically still in the way you might when someone is telling you something so important that you dare not miss a word. Without thinking about it, you'll find yourself leaning forward or nodding your head—gestures that would appear unnatural if you were doing them because you'd been told to.

Of course, listening to and responding to an audience in the middle of your speech requires that you have your material down cold. But you can also take what your listeners tell you and use it to improve future presentations. I worked with a sales executive who had been so successful that she began touring the world in order to share her secrets with others. In listening to audiences, paying attention to their bodies as well as their words, she began to realize that they didn't just want to receive what she had to say; they wanted to give her something in return. The executive's speeches were inspiring, and her listeners wanted to thank her. So we designed a brief but meaningful ceremony near the end of her speech that allowed the audience members to get up, interact with one another, and give back to the speaker some of the inspiration she was giving them.

Consider Carol once again. Because of her intent to pick up on her listeners' emotions, Carol begins to realize over the course of several speeches that she has been wrongly assuming that her salespeople share her sense of urgency about their major competitor. She resolves to spend more time at the beginning of her next presentation explaining why stretch goals are important. This response to her listeners' state of mind, when combined with her own desire to be open, connected, and passionate, strengthens her growing ability to come across as—and be—an authentic speaker.

Originally published in November 2008. Reprint R0811H

Telling Tales

by Stephen Denning

IN 1998, I MADE A pilgrimage to the International Storytelling Center in Jonesborough, Tennessee, seeking some enlightenment. Several years earlier, as the program director of knowledge management at the World Bank, I had stumbled onto the power of storytelling. Despite a career of scoffing at such touchy-feely stuff—like most business executives, I knew that analytical was good, anecdotal was bad—I had changed my thinking because I'd seen stories help galvanize an organization around a defined business goal.

In the mid-1990s, that goal was to get people at the World Bank to support efforts at knowledge management—a pretty foreign notion within the organization at the time. I offered people cogent arguments about the need to gather the knowledge that was scattered throughout the organization. They didn't listen. I gave PowerPoint presentations that compellingly demonstrated the importance of sharing and leveraging this information. My audiences merely looked dazed. In desperation, I was ready to try almost anything.

Then in 1996 I began telling people a story:

In June of 1995, a health worker in a tiny town in Zambia went to the Web site of the Centers for Disease Control and got the answer to a question about the treatment for malaria. Remember that this was in Zambia, one of the poorest countries in the world, and it happened in a tiny place 600 kilometers from the capital city. But the most striking thing about this picture, at least for us, is that the World Bank isn't in it. Despite our know-how on all kinds of poverty-related issues, that knowledge isn't available to the millions of people who could use it. Imagine if it were. Think what an organization we could become.

This simple story helped World Bank staff and managers envision a different kind of future for the organization. When knowledge management later became an official corporate priority, I used similar stories to maintain the momentum. So I began to wonder how the tool of narrative might be put to work even more effectively. Being a typically rational manager, I decided to consult the experts.

At the International Storytelling Center, I told the Zambia story to a professional storyteller, J.G. "Paw-Paw" Pinkerton, and asked the master what he thought. You can imagine my chagrin when he said he didn't hear a story at all. There was no real telling. There was no plot. There was no building up of the characters. Who was this health worker in Zambia? And what was her world like? What did it feel like to be in the exotic environment of Zambia, facing the problems she faced? My anecdote, he said, was a pathetic thing, not a story at all. I needed to start from scratch if I hoped to turn it into a "real story."

Was I surprised? Well, not exactly. The story *was* pretty bland. There was a problem with this advice from the expert, though. I knew in my heart it was wrong. And with that realization, I was on the brink of an important insight: Beware the well-told story!

The Power of Narrative

But let's back up a bit. Do stories really have a role to play in the business world? Believe me, I'm familiar with the skepticism about them. When you talk about "storytelling" to a group of hardheaded executives, you'd better be prepared for some eye rolling. If the group is polite as well as tough, don't be surprised if the eyes simply glaze over.

That's because most executives operate with a particular—and generally justified—mind-set. Analysis is what drives business thinking. It cuts through the fog of myth, gossip, and speculation to get to the hard facts. It goes wherever the observations and premises and conclusions

Idea in Brief

A carefully chosen story can help the leader of an organization translate an abstract concept into a meaningful mandate for employees. The key is to know which narrative strategies are right for what circumstances.

Knowledge management expert Stephen Denning explains that, for optimal effect, form should follow function. Challenging one professional storyteller's view that more is better, Denning points out that it's not always desirable (or practical) to launch into an epic that's jam-packed with complex characters, cleverly placed plot points, an intricate rising action, and a neatly resolved denouement. True, if listeners have time and interest, a narrative-savvy leader can use a vividly rendered tale to promote communication between management and staff, for instance, or even to foster collaboration—especially when the story is emotionally moving. However, if the aim is to motivate people to act when they might not be inclined to

do so, it's best to take an approach that's light on detail. Otherwise, particulars can bog down listeners and prevent them from focusing on the message.

Drawing on his experiences at the World Bank and observations made elsewhere, the author provides several dos and don'ts for organizational storytellers, along with examples of narratives that get results. The sidebar "A Storytelling Catalog" presents seven distinct types of stories, the situations in which they should be told, and tips on how to tell them. Many of these aren't even stories in the "well-told" sense—they run the rhetorical gamut from one-liners to full-blown speeches—but they succeed because they're tailored to fit the situation. So even though it's common in business to favor the analytical over the anecdotal, leaders with the strength to push past some initial skepticism about the enterprise of storytelling will find that the creative effort pays off.

take it, undistorted by the hopes or fears of the analyst. Its strength lies in its objectivity, its impersonality, its heartlessness.

Yet this strength is also a weakness. Analysis might excite the mind, but it hardly offers a route to the heart. And that's where we must go if we are to motivate people not only to take action but to do so with energy and enthusiasm. At a time when corporate survival often requires disruptive change, leadership involves inspiring people to act in unfamiliar, and often unwelcome, ways. Mind-numbing cascades of numbers or daze-inducing PowerPoint slides won't achieve this goal. Even the most logical arguments usually won't do the trick.

But effective storytelling often does. In fact, in certain situations nothing else works. Although good business arguments are developed through the use of numbers, they are typically approved on the basis of a story—that is, a narrative that links a set of events in some kind of causal sequence. Storytelling can translate those dry and abstract numbers into compelling pictures of a leader's goals. I saw this happen at the World Bank—by 2000, we were increasingly recognized as leaders in the area of knowledge management—and have seen it in numerous other large organizations since then.

So why was I having problems with the advice I had received from the professional storyteller in Jonesborough?

A "Poorly Told" Story

The timing of my trip to Tennessee was fortunate. If I had sought expert advice two years earlier, I might have taken the master's recommendations without question. But I'd had some time to approach the idea of organizational storytelling with a beginner's mind, free of strictures about "the right way" to tell a story.

It wasn't that I couldn't follow Paw-Paw Pinkerton's recommendations. I saw immediately how to flesh out my modest anecdote about the health worker in Zambia: You'd dramatically depict her life, the scourge of malaria that she faced in her work, and perhaps the pain and suffering of the patient she was treating that day. You'd describe the extraordinary set of events that had led to her being seated in front of a computer screen deep in the hinterland of Zambia. You'd describe the false leads she had followed before she came across the CDC Web site. You'd build up to the moment of triumph when she found the answer to her question about malaria and vividly describe how that answer was about to transform the life of her patient. The story would be a veritable epic.

This "maximalist" account would be more engrossing than my relatively dry anecdote. But I had learned enough by then to realize that telling the story in this way to a corporate audience would not galvanize implementation of a strange new idea like knowledge management. I knew that in the modern workplace, people had neither the time nor the patience—remember executives' general skepticism about storytelling in the first place—to absorb a richly detailed narrative. If I was going to hold the attention of my audience, I had to make my point in seconds, not in minutes.

There was another problem. Even if my audience did take the time to listen to a fully developed tale, my telling it in that fashion would not allow listeners the mental space to relate the story to their own quite different worlds. Although I was describing a health worker in Zambia, I wanted everyone to focus not on Zambia but on their own situations. I hoped they would think, "If the CDC can reach a health worker in Zambia, why can't the World Bank? Why don't we put our knowledge on the Web and broaden our scope?" But if my listeners were immersed in a saga about that health worker and her patient, they might not have any attention left to ask themselves these questions—or to provide answers. In other words, I didn't want my audience too interested in Zambia. A minimalist narrative was effective, in fact, because it lacked detail and texture. The same characteristic that the professional storyteller saw as a flaw was, for my purposes, a strength.

On my return from Jonesborough, I educated myself about the principles of traditional storytelling. More than 2,000 years ago, Aristotle, in his *Poetics,* said stories should have a beginning, a middle, and an end. They should include complex characters as well as a plot that incorporates a reversal of fortune and a lesson learned. Furthermore, the storyteller should be so engaged with the story— visualizing the action, feeling what the characters feel—that the listeners become drawn into the narrative's world. Aristotle's formula has proved successful over the ages, from *The Arabian Nights* to *The Decameron* to *The Adventures of Tom Sawyer* and most Hollywood screenplays.

Despite the narrative power of the traditional story, I knew that it probably wouldn't spark action in an organization. In retrospect, though, I realize that my insight blinded me to something else. Believing that this wonderful and rich tradition had no place in the

A Storytelling Catalog

STORYTELLING IS AN INCREASINGLY ACCEPTED way to achieve management goals. But leaders need to use a variety of narrative patterns for different aims.

Sparking Action

Leadership is, above all, about getting people to change. To achieve that goal, you need to communicate the sometimes complex nature of the changes required and inspire an often skeptical organization to enthusiastically carry them out. This is the place for what I call a "springboard story," one that enables listeners to visualize the transformation needed in their circumstances and then to act on that realization.

Such a story is based on an actual event, preferably recent enough to seem relevant. It has a single protagonist with whom members of the target audience can identify. And there is an authentically happy ending, in which a change has at least in part been successfully implemented. (There is also an implicit alternate ending, an unhappy one that would have resulted had the change not occurred.)

The story has enough detail to be intelligible and credible but—and this is key—not so much texture that the audience becomes completely wrapped up in it. If that happens, people won't have the mental space to create an analogous scenario for change in their own organization. For example, if you want to get an organization to embrace a new technology, you might tell stories about individuals elsewhere who have successfully implemented it, without dwelling on the specifics.

Communicating Who You Are

You aren't likely to lead people through wrenching change if they don't trust you. And if they're to trust you, they have to know you: who you are, where you've come from, and why you hold the views you do. Ideally, they'll end up not only understanding you but also empathizing with you.

Stories for this purpose are usually based on a life event that reveals some strength or vulnerability and shows what the speaker took from the experience. For example, Jack Welch's success in making General Electric a winner was undoubtedly aided by his ability to tell his own story, which includes a tongue-lashing he once received from his mother after he hurled a hockey stick across the ice in response to a disappointing loss. "You punk!" she said, as Welch tells it in his memoir *Jack: Straight from the Gut*. "If you don't know how to lose, you'll never know how to win."

Unlike a story designed to spark action, this kind is typically well told, with colorful detail and context. So the speaker needs to ensure that the audience has enough time and interest to hear the story.

Transmitting Values

Stories can be effective tools for ingraining values within an organization, particularly those that help forestall problems by clearly establishing limits on destructive behavior. A story of this type ensures that the audience understands "how things are done around here."

These narratives often take the form of a parable. Religious leaders have used them for thousands of years to communicate values. The stories are usually set in some kind of generic past and have few context-setting details—though the context needs to seem relevant to the listeners. The "facts" of such tales can be hypothetical, but they must be believable. For example, a story might tell the sad fate of someone who failed to see the conflict of interest in not disclosing his or her financial interest in a company supplier.

Of course, narratives alone cannot establish values in an organization. Leaders need to live the values on a daily basis.

Fostering Collaboration

Every management textbook talks about the value of getting people to work together. But the only advice most of them offer on making that happen in real-life work environments is "Encourage conversations." Yes, but how?

One approach is to generate a common narrative around a group's concerns and goals, beginning with a story told by one member of the group. Ideally, that first story sparks another, which sparks another. If the process continues, group members develop a shared perspective, one that creates a sense of community. The first story must be emotionally moving enough to unleash the narrative impulse in others and to create a readiness to hear more stories. It could, for example, vividly describe how the speaker had grappled with a difficult work situation.

For this process to occur, it is best if the group has an open agenda that allows the stories to surface organically. It is also desirable to have a plan ready so that the energy generated by the positive experience of sharing stories can be immediately channeled into action.

Taming the Grapevine

Rumors flow incessantly through every organization. "Have you heard the latest?" is a refrain that's difficult for managers to deal with. Denying a rumor can give it credibility. Asking how it got started can ensure its spread. Ignoring it risks allowing it to spiral out of control. Rumors about issues central to the future of the organization—takeovers, reorganizations, major managerial changes—can be an enormous distraction (or worse) to employees. So as an executive, what can you do? One response is to harness the energy of the

(continued)

A Storytelling Catalog (continued)

If your objective is:	You will need a story that:	In telling it, you will need to:	Your story will inspire such responses as:
Sparking action	Describes how a successful change was implemented in the past, but allows listeners to imagine how it might work in their situation.	Avoid excessive detail that will take the audience's mind off its own challenge.	"Just imagine . . ." "What if . . ."
Communicating who you are	Provides audience-engaging drama and reveals some strength or vulnerability from your past.	Include meaningful details, but also make sure the audience has the time and inclination to hear your story.	"I didn't know that about him!" "Now I see what she's driving at."
Transmitting values	Feels familiar to the audience and will prompt discussion about the issues raised by the value being promoted.	Use believable (though perhaps hypothetical) characters and situations, and never forget that the story must be consistent with your own actions.	"That's so right!" "Why don't we do that all the time?"
Fostering collaboration	Movingly recounts a situation that listeners have also experienced and that prompts them to share their own stories about the topic.	Ensure that a set agenda doesn't squelch this swapping of stories—and that you have an action plan ready to tap the energy unleashed by this narrative chain reaction.	"That reminds me of the time that I . . ." "Hey, I've got a story like that."
Taming the grapevine	Highlights, often through the use of gentle humor, some aspect of a rumor that reveals it to be untrue or unlikely.	Avoid the temptation to be mean-spirited, and be sure that the rumor is indeed false.	"No kidding!" "I'd never thought about it like that before!"

Sharing knowledge	Focuses on mistakes made and shows in some detail how they were corrected, with an explanation of why the solution worked.	Solicit alternative—and possibly better—solutions.	"There but for the grace of God . . ." "Wow! We'd better watch that from now on."
Leading people into the future	Evokes the future you want to create without providing excessive detail that will only turn out to be wrong.	Be sure of your storytelling skills. (Otherwise, use a story in which the past can serve as a springboard to the future.)	"When do we start?" "Let's do it!"

grapevine to defuse the rumor, using a story to convince listeners that the gossip is either untrue or unreasonable. This kind of story highlights the incongruity between the rumor and reality. You could use gentle satire to mock the rumor, the rumor's author, or even yourself, in an effort to under-mine the rumor's power. For example, you might deal with a false rumor of "imminent companywide reorganization" by jokingly recounting how the front office's current struggles involving the seating chart for executive committee meetings would have to be worked out first. Keep in mind, though, that humor can backfire. Mean-spirited teasing can generate a well-deserved backlash.

The trick is to work with, not against, the flow of the vast underground river of informal communication that exists in every organization. Of course, you can't ridicule a rumor into oblivion if it's true or at least reasonable. If that's the case, there is little you can do but admit the substance of the rumor, put it in perspective, and move on.

Sharing Knowledge

Much of the intellectual capital of an organization is not written down anywhere but resides in people's minds. Communicating this know-how across an orga-nization and beyond typically occurs informally, through the sharing of stories.

Knowledge-sharing narratives are unusual in that they lack a hero or even a detectable plot. They are more about problems, and how and why they got—or, more likely, didn't get—resolved. They include a description of the

(continued)

A Storytelling Catalog (continued)

problem, the setting, and the solution. Because they highlight a problem—say, the challenge employees face in learning to use a new system—they tend to have a negative tone. And because they often focus in detail on why a particular solution worked, they may be of little interest outside a defined group of people. Though unashamedly unentertaining and lacking most elements of a conventional story, they are nonetheless the uncelebrated workhorse of organizational narrative.

They present a difficulty, however. In a corporate setting, stories about problems don't flow easily, not only because people fear the consequences of admitting mistakes, but also because, in the flush of success, people tend to forget what they learned along the way. As a result, the knowledge-sharing story cannot be compelled; it has to be teased out. That is, a discussion of successes may be needed in order to get people to talk about what has gone wrong and how it can be fixed.

Leading People into the Future

An important part of a leader's job is preparing others for what lies ahead, whether in the concrete terms of an actual scenario or the more conceptual

---

time-constrained world of modern business was as wrongheaded as thinking that all stories had to be full of detail and color. I would later see that the well-told story is relevant in a modern organization. Indeed, a number of surprises about the use of storytelling in organizations awaited me.

Tales of Success and Failure

In December 2000, I left the World Bank and began to consult with companies on their knowledge management and, by extension, their use of organizational stories. As part of this work, I once found myself in London with Dave Snowden, a director of IBM's Institute of Knowledge Management, teaching a master class on storytelling to around 70 executives from private- and public-sector organizations.

During the class's morning session, I spoke about my experience at the World Bank and how a positive orientation was essential if a narrative like the one about Zambia was to be effective. But in the

terms of a vision. A story can help take listeners from where they are now to where they need to be, by making them comfortable with an image of the future. The problem, of course, lies in crafting a credible narrative about the future when the future is unknowable.

Thus, if such stories are to serve their purpose, they should whet listeners' imaginative appetite about the future without providing detail that will likely turn out to be inaccurate. Listeners should be able to remold the story in their minds as the future unfolds with all its unexpected twists and turns. And clearly, the story should portray that state in a positive way: People are more likely to overcome uncertainty about change if they are shown what to aim for rather than what to avoid.

Note that telling an evocative narrative about the future requires a high degree of verbal skill, something not every leader possesses. But the spring-board story, described above, provides an alternative. Hearing about a change that has already happened elsewhere can help listeners to imagine how it might play out for them in the future.

afternoon, to my dismay, my fellow presenter emphatically asserted the opposite. At IBM and elsewhere, Dave had found purely positive stories to be problematic. They were, he said, like the Janet and John children's stories in the United Kingdom or the Dick and Jane stories in the United States: The characters were so good they made you feel queasy. The naughtiest thing Janet and John would do was spill a bottle of water in the yard. Then they would go and tell their mother about it and promise never to do it again. Janet would volunteer to help out with the cleanup and John would offer to help wash the car. These stories for children reflected a desire to show things as they should be rather than as they are. In a corporate environment, Dave told his audience, listeners would respond to such rosy tales by conjuring up negative "antistories" about what must have actually happened. His message: Beware the positive story!

After the workshop, Dave and I discussed why his stories focused on the negative while mine accentuated the positive. I could see he had a point, that negative stories can be more powerful than positive ones. I'd used negative stories myself when trying to teach people the nitty-gritty of any subject. The fact is, people learn more from their mistakes than from their successes.

Eventually, however, it dawned on me that our points of view were complementary and that our stories served different purposes: My stories were crafted to motivate people, and Dave's were designed to share knowledge. His stories might describe how and why a team failed to accomplish an objective, with the aim of helping others avoid the same mistakes. (To elicit such stories, Dave often had to start by getting people to talk about their successes, even if these accounts were ultimately less useful vehicles for conveying knowledge.) It was then I began to realize that the purpose of telling a story might determine its form.

Granted, even optimistic stories have to be true and believable, since jaded corporate audiences know too well the experience of being presented with half-truths. Stories told in order to spur action need to make good on their promises and contain sufficient evidence of a positive outcome. But stories intended mainly to transfer knowledge must be more than true. Because their objective is to generate understanding and not action, they tend to highlight the pitfalls of ignorance; they are meant not to inspire people but to make them cautious. Just as the minimalist stories that I told to spark action were different from traditional entertainment stories, so effective knowledge-sharing stories would have negative rather than positive overtones.

A Collective Yawn

Once I saw that different narrative forms could further different business goals, I looked for other ways that managers could make stories work for them. A number of distinct story types began to emerge—ones that didn't necessarily follow Aristotelian guidelines but were nonetheless used to good effect in a variety of organizations. (For descriptions of some of them and the purposes for which they might be used, see the sidebar "A Storytelling Catalog.") I continued to come across unexpected insights about the nature of storytelling within organizations.

For instance, if negative stories have their place, so do "boring" ones. In his book *Talking about Machines,* Julian Orr recounts a number of stories that have circulated among Xerox repair technicians. While rich in detail, they are even less storylike than my little anecdote about the health care worker in Zambia. Most of these tales, which present solutions to technical problems, lack a plot and a distinct character. In fact, they are hardly stories at all, with little to hold the interest of anyone except those close to the often esoteric subject matter. Why are they compelling even to this limited audience? Because they are driven by a detailed explanation of the cause-and-effect relationship between an action and its consequence. For example:

> You've got a malfunctioning copy machine with an E053 error code, which is supposed to mean a problem in the 24-volt Interlock Power Supply. But you could chase the source of that 24-volt Interlock problem forever, and you'd never, ever find out what it is. If you're lucky enough, you'll eventually get an F066 error code, which indicates the true source of the malfunction—namely, a shorted dicorotron. Apparently, this is happening because the circuitry in the XER board has been changed to prevent the damage that would otherwise occur when a dicorotron shorted. Before the change in circuitry, a shorted dicorotron would have fried the whole XER board. Changing the circuitry has prevented damage to the XER board, but it's created a different issue. Now an E053 error message doesn't give you the true source of the machine's malfunction.

This story, slightly condensed here, doesn't just describe the technician's accurate diagnosis of a problem; it also relates why things happened as they did. So the account, negative in tone and almost unintelligible to an outsider, is both informative and interesting to its intended audience.

As I continued my investigation, one area of particular interest to me was the link between storytelling and leadership. I already knew from personal experience how stories could be used as a catalyst for organizational action. And I had read in two influential books about leadership—*Leading Minds* by Howard Gardner and *The Leadership Engine* by Noel Tichy—how stories could help leaders define their personality for their followers, boosting others' confidence in the leaders' integrity and providing some idea of how they might act in a given situation.

I also had seen leaders using narrative to inculcate a positive set of corporate values and beliefs in the hearts and minds of their employees. Think, for example, of Tyco's effort to repair its battered value system. The company began by creating a straightforward manual that outlined new rules in such areas as sexual harassment, conflicts of interest, and fraud. But Eric Pillmore, senior vice president of corporate governance, quickly figured out that, as written, the booklet would merely gather dust on people's shelves. So he threw out what he had done and started again in an attempt to bring the principles alive through narrative. The story below became part of the revised guide, as a sidebar in the section on sexual harassment and other forms of intimidating behavior in the workplace:

> The entire team jokes about Tom being gay. Tom has never complained and doesn't seem to mind, but when Mark is assigned to work with Tom, the jokes turn on Mark. Now that Mark receives the brunt of the jokes, he tells his supervisor he wants to be reassigned. His supervisor complies with Mark's request.

While the guide clearly lays out the company's policy on harassment, the simple narrative helps bring the policy to life and provides a starting point for thinking about and discussing the complex issues involved. Dozens of similar stories illustrate an array of company policies.

An Enticing but Hazy Future

Although these types of stories furthered leadership goals in a relatively predictable way, others I came across were more quirky—particularly ones used to communicate vision. Noel Tichy writes in

The Leadership Engine about the importance of preparing an organization for change. He notes that "the best way to get humans to venture into unknown terrain is to make that terrain familiar and desirable by taking them there first in their imaginations." Aha! I thought. Here is a place where storytelling, perhaps the most powerful route to people's imaginations, could prove indispensable.

But as I looked at examples of such stories in a number of arenas, I discovered that most of the successful ones were surprisingly sketchy about the details of the imagined future. Consider Winston Churchill's "We Shall Fight on the Beaches" speech and Martin Luther King, Jr.'s "I Have a Dream" speech. Neither of these famous addresses came close to describing the future in enough detail that it became, in listeners' minds, "familiar terrain."

Over time—and, in part, through my work in corporate scenario planning—I realized why. Specific predictions about the future are likely to be proved wrong. Because such predictions almost inevitably differ in major or minor ways from what eventually happens, leaders who proclaim them risk losing people's confidence. Consequently, a story designed to prepare people for change needs to evoke the future and conjure up a direction for getting there—but without being too precise. Think of the corporate future that was laid out in a famous mandate by Jack Welch: "General Electric will be either number one or number two in the field, or we will exit the sector." This is a clear, but general, description of where Welch wanted to take the company. Like my Zambia story, although for different reasons, this statement doesn't convey *too* much information.

I also came across stories used in somewhat unusual situations that called for reactive rather than proactive measures. These stories counteracted negative ones that circulated like a virus within an organization and threatened to infect the entire body. Dave Snowden of IBM first pointed out to me how stories could be used in this manner. His hypothesis was that you could attach a positive story to a negative one in order to defuse it, as an antibody would neutralize an antigen.

For example, at an IBM manufacturing site for laptop computers in the United Kingdom, stories circulated among the blue-collar workers about the facility's managers, who were accused of "not doing any real work," "being overpaid," and "having no idea what it's like on the manufacturing line." But an additional story was injected into the mix: One day, a new site director turned up in a white coat, unannounced and unaccompanied, and sat on the line making ThinkPads. He asked workers on the assembly line for help. In response, someone asked him, "Why do you earn so much more than I do?" His simple reply: "If you screw up badly, you lose your job. If I screw up badly, 3,000 people lose their jobs."

While not a story in the traditional sense, the manager's words—and actions—served as a seed for the story that eventually circulated in opposition to the one about managers' being lazy and overpaid. You can imagine the buzz: "Blimey, you should've seen how he fumbled with those circuit boards. I guess *he'll* never work on the line. But you know, he does have a point about his pay." The atmosphere at the facility began improving within weeks.

Much work remains to be done in developing a menu of narrative patterns that can be used for different purposes in an organizational setting. Although the handful of story types that I've identified is no more than a start, I hope it inspires leaders to consider the various ways storytelling might be used. Certainly, the ability to tell the right story at the right time is emerging as an essential leadership skill, one that can help managers cope with, and get business results in, the turbulent world of the twenty-first century.

Originally published in May 2004. Reprint R0405H

How to Pitch a Brilliant Idea

by Kimberly D. Elsbach

COMING UP WITH CREATIVE IDEAS is easy; selling them to strangers is hard. All too often, entrepreneurs, sales executives, and marketing managers go to great lengths to show how their new business plans or creative concepts are practical and high margin—only to be rejected by corporate decision makers who don't seem to understand the real value of the ideas. Why does this happen?

It turns out that the problem has as much to do with the seller's traits as with an idea's inherent quality. The person on the receiving end tends to gauge the pitcher's creativity as well as the proposal itself. And judgments about the pitcher's ability to come up with workable ideas can quickly and permanently overshadow perceptions of the idea's worth. We all like to think that people judge us carefully and objectively on our merits. But the fact is, they rush to place us into neat little categories—they stereotype us. So the first thing to realize when you're preparing to make a pitch to strangers is that your audience is going to put you into a box. And they're going to do it really fast. Research suggests that humans can categorize others in less than 150 milliseconds. Within 30 minutes, they've made lasting judgments about your character.

These insights emerged from my lengthy study of the $50 billion U.S. film and television industry. Specifically, I worked with 50 Hollywood executives involved in assessing pitches from screenwriters.

Over the course of six years, I observed dozens of 30-minute pitches in which the screenwriters encountered the "catchers" for the first time. In interviewing and observing the pitchers and catchers, I was able to discern just how quickly assessments of creative potential are made in these high-stakes exchanges. (The deals that arise as a result of successful screenplay pitches are often multimillion-dollar projects, rivaling in scope the development of new car models by Detroit's largest automakers and marketing campaigns by New York's most successful advertising agencies.) To determine whether my observations applied to business settings beyond Hollywood, I attended a variety of product-design, marketing, and venture-capital pitch sessions and conducted interviews with executives responsible for judging creative, high-stakes ideas from pitchers previously unknown to them. In those environments, the results were remarkably similar to what I had seen in the movie business.

People on the receiving end of pitches have no formal, verifiable, or objective measures for assessing that elusive trait, creativity. Catchers—even the expert ones—therefore apply a set of subjective and often inaccurate criteria very early in the encounter, and from that point on, the tone is set. If a catcher detects subtle cues indicating that the pitcher isn't creative, the proposal is toast. But that's not the whole story. I've discovered that catchers tend to respond well if they are made to feel that they are participating in an idea's development.

The pitchers who do this successfully are those who tend to be categorized by catchers into one of three prototypes. I call them the *showrunner,* the *artist,* and the *neophyte*. Showrunners come off as professionals who combine creative inspiration with production know-how. Artists appear to be quirky and unpolished and to prefer the world of creative ideas to quotidian reality. Neophytes tend to be—or act as if they were—young, inexperienced, and naive. To involve the audience in the creative process, showrunners deliberately level the power differential between themselves and their catchers; artists invert the differential; and neophytes exploit it. If you're a pitcher, the bottom-line implication is this: By successfully projecting yourself as one of the three creative types and getting your catcher to view himself or herself

Idea in Brief

Coming up with creative ideas is easy; selling them to strangers is hard. Entrepreneurs, sales executives, and marketing managers often go to great lengths to demonstrate how their new concepts are practical and profitable—only to be rejected by corporate decision makers who don't seem to understand the value of the ideas. Why does this happen?

Having studied Hollywood executives who assess screenplay pitches, the author says the person on the receiving end—the "catcher"—tends to gauge the pitcher's creativity as well as the proposal itself. An impression of the pitcher's ability to come up with workable ideas can quickly and permanently overshadow the catcher's feelings about an idea's worth. To determine whether these observations apply to business settings beyond Hollywood, the author attended product design, marketing, and venture-capital pitch sessions and conducted interviews with executives responsible for judging new ideas. The results in those environments were similar to her observations in Hollywood, she says.

Catchers subconsciously categorize successful pitchers as *showrunners* (smooth and professional), *artists* (quirky and unpolished), or *neophytes* (inexperienced and naive). The research also reveals that catchers tend to respond well when they believe they are participating in an idea's development. As Oscar-winning writer, director, and producer Oliver Stone puts it, screenwriters pitching an idea should "pull back and project what he needs onto your idea in order to make the story whole for him."

To become a successful pitcher, portray yourself as one of the three creative types and engage your catchers in the creative process. By finding ways to give your catchers a chance to shine, you sell yourself as a likable collaborator.

as a creative collaborator, you can improve your chances of selling an idea.

My research also has implications for those who buy ideas: Catchers should beware of relying on stereotypes. It's all too easy to be dazzled by pitchers who ultimately can't get their projects off the ground, and it's just as easy to overlook the creative individuals who can make good on their ideas. That's why it's important for the catcher to test every pitcher, a matter we'll return to in the following pages.

The Sorting Hat

In the late 1970s, psychologists Nancy Cantor and Walter Mischel, then at Stanford University, demonstrated that we all use sets of stereotypes—what they called "person prototypes"—to categorize strangers in the first moments of interaction. Though such instant typecasting is arguably unfair, pattern matching is so firmly hardwired into human psychology that only conscious discipline can counteract it.

Yale University creativity researcher Robert Sternberg contends that the prototype matching we use to assess originality in others results from our implicit belief that creative people possess certain traits—unconventionality, for example, as well as intuitiveness, sensitivity, narcissism, passion, and perhaps youth. We develop these stereotypes through direct and indirect experiences with people known to be creative, from personally interacting with the 15-year-old guitar player next door to hearing stories about Pablo Picasso.

When a person we don't know pitches an idea to us, we search for visual and verbal matches with those implicit models, remembering only the characteristics that identify the pitcher as one type or another. We subconsciously award points to people we can easily identify as having creative traits; we subtract points from those who are hard to assess or who fit negative stereotypes.

In hurried business situations in which executives must evaluate dozens of ideas in a week, or even a day, catchers are rarely willing to expend the effort necessary to judge an idea more objectively. Like Harry Potter's Sorting Hat, they classify pitchers in a matter of seconds. They use negative stereotyping to rapidly identify the no-go ideas. All you have to do is fall into one of four common negative stereotypes, and the pitch session will be over before it has begun. (For more on these stereotypes, see the sidebar "How to Kill Your Own Pitch.") In fact, many such sessions are strictly a process of elimination; in my experience, only 1% of ideas make it beyond the initial pitch.

Unfortunately for pitchers, type-based elimination is easy, because negative impressions tend to be more salient and memorable than positive ones. To avoid fast elimination, successful pitchers—only

25% of those I have observed—turn the tables on the catchers by enrolling them in the creative process. These pitchers exude passion for their ideas and find ways to give catchers a chance to shine. By doing so, they induce the catchers to judge them as likable collaborators. Oscar-winning writer, director, and producer Oliver Stone told me that the invitation to collaborate on an idea is a "seduction." His advice to screenwriters pitching an idea to a producer is to "pull back and project what he needs onto your idea in order to make the story whole for him." The three types of successful pitchers have their own techniques for doing this, as we'll see.

The Showrunner

In the corporate world, as in Hollywood, showrunners combine creative thinking and passion with what Sternberg and Todd Lubart, authors of *Defying the Crowd: Cultivating Creativity in a Culture of Conformity,* call "practical intelligence"—a feel for which ideas are likely to contribute to the business. Showrunners tend to display charisma and wit in pitching, say, new design concepts to marketing, but they also demonstrate enough technical know-how to convince catchers that the ideas can be developed according to industry-standard practices and within resource constraints. Though they may not have the most or the best ideas, showrunners are those rare people in organizations who see the majority of their concepts fully implemented.

An example of a showrunner is the legendary kitchen-gadget inventor and pitchman Ron Popeil. Perfectly coiffed and handsome, Popeil is a combination design master and ringmaster. In his *New Yorker* account of Popeil's phenomenally successful Ronco Showtime Rotisserie & BBQ, Malcolm Gladwell described how Popeil fuses entertainment skills—he enthusiastically showcases the product as an innovation that will "change your life"—with business savvy. For his television spots, Popeil makes sure that the chickens are roasted to exactly the resplendent golden brown that looks best on camera. And he designed the rotisserie's glass front to reduce glare, so that to the home cook, the revolving, dripping chickens look just as they do on TV.

How to Kill Your Own Pitch

BEFORE YOU EVEN GET TO the stage in the pitch where the catcher categorizes you as a particular creative type, you have to avoid some dangerous pigeonholes: the four negative stereotypes that are guaranteed to kill a pitch. And take care, because negative cues carry more weight than positive ones.

The pushover would rather unload an idea than defend it. ("I could do one of these in red, or if you don't like that, I could do it in blue.") One venture capitalist I spoke with offered the example of an entrepreneur who was seeking funding for a computer networking start-up. When the VCs raised concerns about an aspect of the device, the pitcher simply offered to remove it from the design, leading the investors to suspect that the pitcher didn't really care about his idea.

The robot presents a proposal too formulaically, as if it had been memorized from a how-to book. Witness the entrepreneur who responds to prospective investors' questions about due diligence and other business details with canned answers from his PowerPoint talk.

The first Hollywood pitcher I observed was a showrunner. The minute he walked into the room, he scored points with the studio executive as a creative type, in part because of his new, pressed jeans, his fashionable black turtleneck, and his nice sport coat. The clean hair draping his shoulders showed no hint of gray. He had come to pitch a weekly television series based on the legend of Robin Hood. His experience as a marketer was apparent; he opened by mentioning an earlier TV series of his that had been based on a comic book. The pitcher remarked that the series had enjoyed some success as a marketing franchise, spawning lunch boxes, bath toys, and action figures.

Showrunners create a level playing field by engaging the catcher in a kind of knowledge duet. They typically begin by getting the catcher to respond to a memory or some other subject with which the showrunner is familiar. Consider this give-and-take:

Pitcher: Remember Errol Flynn's *Robin Hood*?

Catcher: Oh, yeah. One of my all-time favorites as a kid.

Pitcher: Yes, it was classic. Then, of course, came Costner's version.

The used-car salesman is that obnoxious, argumentative character too often deployed in consultancies and corporate sales departments. One vice president of marketing told me the story of an arrogant consultant who put in a proposal to her organization. The consultant's offer was vaguely intriguing, and she asked him to revise his bid slightly. Instead of working with her, he argued with her. Indeed, he tried selling the same package again and again, each time arguing why his proposal would produce the most astonishing bottom-line results the company had ever seen. In the end, she grew so tired of his wheedling insistence and inability to listen courteously to her feedback that she told him she wasn't interested in seeing any more bids from him.

The charity case is needy; all he or she wants is a job. I recall a freelance consultant who had developed a course for executives on how to work with independent screenwriters. He could be seen haunting the halls of production companies, knocking on every open door, giving the same pitch. As soon as he sensed he was being turned down, he began pleading with the catcher, saying he really, *really* needed to fill some slots to keep his workshop going.

Catcher: That was much darker. And it didn't evoke as much passion as the original.

Pitcher: But the special effects were great.

Catcher: Yes, they were.

Pitcher: That's the twist I want to include in this new series.

Catcher: Special effects?

Pitcher: We're talking a science fiction version of *Robin Hood*. Robin has a sorcerer in his band of merry men who can conjure up all kinds of scary and wonderful spells.

Catcher: I love it!

The pitcher sets up his opportunity by leading the catcher through a series of shared memories and viewpoints. Specifically, he engages the catcher by asking him to recall and comment on familiar movies. With each response, he senses and then builds on the catcher's knowledge and interest, eventually guiding the catcher to the core idea by using a word ("twist") that's common to the vocabularies of both producers and screenwriters.

Showrunners also display an ability to improvise, a quality that allows them to adapt if a pitch begins to go awry. Consider the dynamic between the creative director of an ad agency and a prospective client, a major television sports network. As Mallorre Dill reported in a 2001 *Adweek* article on award-winning advertising campaigns, the network's VP of marketing was seeking help with a new campaign for coverage of the upcoming professional basketball season, and the ad agency was invited to make a pitch. Prior to the meeting, the network executive stressed to the agency that the campaign would have to appeal to local markets across the United States while achieving "street credibility" with avid fans.

The agency's creative director and its art director pitched the idea of digitally inserting two average teenagers into video of an NBA game. Initially, the catcher frowned on the idea, wondering aloud if viewers would find it arrogant and aloof. So the agency duo ad-libbed a rap that one teen could recite after scoring on all-star Shaquille O'Neal: "I'm fresh like a can of picante. And I'm deeper than Dante in the circles of hell." The catcher was taken aback at first; then he laughed. Invited to participate in the impromptu rap session, the catcher began inserting his own lines. When the fun was over, the presenters repitched their idea with a slight variation—inserting the teenagers into videos of home-team games for local markets—and the account was sold to the tune of hundreds of thousands of dollars.

Real showrunners are rare—only 20% of the successful pitchers I observed would qualify. Consequently, they are in high demand, which is good news for pitchers who can demonstrate the right combination of talent and expertise.

The Artist

Artists, too, display single-minded passion and enthusiasm about their ideas, but they are less slick and conformist in their dress and mannerisms, and they tend to be shy or socially awkward. As one

Hollywood producer told me, "The more shy a writer seems, the better you think the writing is, because you assume they're living in their internal world." Unlike showrunners, artists appear to have little or no knowledge of, or even interest in, the details of implementation. Moreover, they invert the power differential by completely commanding the catcher's imagination. Instead of engaging the catcher in a duet, they put the audience in thrall to the content. Artists are particularly adept at conducting what physicists call "thought experiments," inviting the audience into imaginary worlds.

One young screenwriter I observed fit the artist type to perfection. He wore black leather pants and a torn T-shirt, several earrings in each ear, and a tattoo on his slender arm. His hair was rumpled, his expression was brooding: Van Gogh meets Tim Burton. He cared little about the production details for the dark, violent cartoon series he imagined; rather, he was utterly absorbed by the unfolding story. He opened his pitch like this: "Picture what happens when a bullet explodes inside someone's brain. Imagine it in slow motion. There is the shattering blast, the tidal wave of red, the acrid smell of gunpowder. That's the opening scene in this animated sci-fi flick." He then proceeded to lead his catchers through an exciting, detailed narrative of his film, as a master storyteller would. At the end, the executives sat back, smiling, and told the writer they'd like to go ahead with his idea.

In the business world, artists are similarly nonconformist. Consider Alan, a product designer at a major packaged-foods manufacturer. I observed Alan in a meeting with business-development executives he'd never met. He had come to pitch an idea based on the premise that children like to play with their food. The proposal was for a cereal with pieces that interlocked in such a way that children could use them for building things, Legos style. With his pocket-protected laboratory coat and horn-rimmed glasses, Alan looked very much the absent-minded professor. As he entered the conference room where the suited-and-tied executives at his company had assembled, he hung back, apparently uninterested in the PowerPoint slides or the marketing and revenue projections of the business-development experts. His appearance and reticence spoke volumes about him. His type was unmistakable.

When it was Alan's turn, he dumped four boxes of prototype cereal onto the mahogany conference table, to the stunned silence of the executives. Ignoring protocol, he began constructing an elaborate fort, all the while talking furiously about the qualities of the corn flour that kept the pieces and the structure together. Finally, he challenged the executives to see who could build the tallest tower. The executives so enjoyed the demonstration that they greenlighted Alan's project.

While artists—who constituted about 40% of the successful pitchers I observed—are not as polished as showrunners, they are the most creative of the three types. Unlike showrunners and neophytes, artists are fairly transparent. It's harder to fake the part. In other words, they don't play to type; they *are* the type. Indeed, it is very difficult for someone who is not an artist to pretend to be one, because genuineness is what makes the artist credible.

The Neophyte

Neophytes are the opposite of showrunners. Instead of displaying their expertise, they plead ignorance. Neophytes score points for daring to do the impossible, something catchers see as refreshing. Unencumbered by tradition or past successes, neophytes present themselves as eager learners. They consciously exploit the power differential between pitcher and catcher by asking directly and boldly for help—not in a desperate way, but with the confidence of a brilliant favorite, a talented student seeking sage advice from a beloved mentor.

Consider the case of one neophyte pitcher I observed, a young, ebullient screenwriter who had just returned from his first trip to Japan. He wanted to develop a show about an American kid (like himself) who travels to Japan to learn to play *taiko* drums, and he brought his drums and sticks into the pitch session. The fellow looked as though he had walked off the set of *Doogie Howser, M.D.* With his infectious smile, he confided to his catchers that he was not going to pitch them a typical show, "mainly because I've never done one. But I think my inexperience here might be a blessing."

He showed the catchers a variety of drumming moves, then asked one person in his audience to help him come up with potential camera angles—such as looking out from inside the drum or viewing it from overhead—inquiring how these might play on the screen. When the catcher got down on his hands and knees to show the neophyte a particularly "cool" camera angle, the pitch turned into a collaborative teaching session. Ignoring his lunch appointment, the catcher spent the next half hour offering suggestions for weaving the story of the young drummer into a series of taiko performances in which artistic camera angles and imaginative lighting and sound would be used to mirror the star's emotions.

Many entrepreneurs are natural neophytes. Lou and Sophie McDermott, two sisters from Australia, started the Savage Sisters sportswear line in the late 1990s. Former gymnasts with petite builds and spunky personalities, they cartwheeled into the clothing business with no formal training in fashion or finance. Instead, they relied heavily on their enthusiasm and optimism and a keen curiosity about the fine points of retailing to get a start in the highly competitive world of teen fashion. On their shopping outings at local stores, the McDermott sisters studied merchandising and product placement—all the while asking store owners how they got started, according to the short documentary film *Cutting Their Own Cloth*.

The McDermott sisters took advantage of their inexperience to learn all they could. They would ask a store owner to give them a tour of the store, and they would pose dozens of questions: "Why do you buy this line and not the other one? Why do you put this dress here and not there? What are your customers like? What do they ask for most?" Instead of being annoying, the McDermotts were charming, friendly, and fun, and the flattered retailers enjoyed being asked to share their knowledge. Once they had struck up a relationship with a retailer, the sisters would offer to bring in samples for the store to test. Eventually, the McDermotts parlayed what they had learned into enough knowledge to start their own retail line. By engaging the store owners as teachers, the McDermotts were able to build a network of expert mentors who wanted to see the neophytes win. Thus neophytes, who constitute about 40% of successful pitchers, achieve their gains largely by sheer force of personality.

Which of the three types is most likely to succeed? Overwhelmingly, catchers look for showrunners, though artists and neophytes can win the day through enchantment and charm. From the catcher's perspective, however, showrunners can also be the most dangerous of all pitchers, because they are the most likely to blind through glitz.

Catchers Beware

When business executives ask me for my insights about creativity in Hollywood, one of the first questions they put to me is, "Why is there so much bad television?" After hearing the stories I've told here, they know the answer: Hollywood executives too often let themselves be wooed by positive stereotypes—particularly that of the showrunner—rather than by the quality of the ideas. Indeed, individuals who become adept at conveying impressions of creative potential, while lacking the real thing, may gain entry into organizations and reach prominence there based on their social influence and impression-management skills, to the catchers' detriment.

Real creativity isn't so easily classified. Researchers such as Sternberg and Lubart have found that people's implicit theories regarding the attributes of creative individuals are off the mark. Furthermore, studies have identified numerous personal attributes that facilitate practical creative behavior. For example, cognitive flexibility, a penchant for diversity, and an orientation toward problem solving are signs of creativity; it simply isn't true that creative types can't be down-to-earth.

Those who buy ideas, then, need to be aware that relying too heavily on stereotypes can cause them to overlook creative individuals who can truly deliver the goods. In my interviews with studio executives and agents, I heard numerous tales of people who had developed reputations as great pitchers but who had trouble producing usable scripts. The same thing happens in business. One well-known example occurred in 1985, when Coca-Cola announced it was changing the Coke formula. Based on pitches from market researchers who had tested the sweeter, Pepsi-like "new Coke" in numerous focus groups, the company's top management decided that the new formula could effectively compete with Pepsi. The idea was a marketing disaster, of course. There was a huge backlash, and the company was forced to reintroduce the old Coke. In a later discussion of the case and the importance of relying on decision makers who are both good pitchers and industry experts, Roberto Goizueta, Coca-Cola's CEO at the time, said to a group of MBAs, in effect, that there's nothing so dangerous as a good pitcher with no real talent.

If a catcher senses that he or she is being swept away by a positive stereotype match, it's important to test the pitcher. Fortunately, assessing the various creative types is not difficult. In a meeting with a showrunner, for example, the catcher can test the pitcher's expertise and probe into past experiences, just as a skilled job interviewer would, and ask how the pitcher would react to various changes to his or her idea. As for artists and neophytes, the best way to judge their ability is to ask them to deliver a finished product. In Hollywood, smart catchers ask artists and neophytes for finished scripts before hiring them. These two types may be unable to deliver specifics about costs or implementation, but a prototype can allow the catcher to judge quality, and it can provide a concrete basis for further discussion. Finally, it's important to enlist the help of other people in vetting pitchers. Another judge or two can help a catcher weigh the pitcher's—and the idea's—pros and cons and help safeguard against hasty judgments.

One CEO of a Northern California design firm looks beyond the obvious earmarks of a creative type when hiring a new designer. She does this by asking not only about successful projects but also about work that failed and what the designer learned from the failures. That way, she can find out whether the prospect is capable of absorbing lessons well and rolling with the punches of an unpredictable work environment. The CEO also asks job prospects what they collect and read, as well as what inspires them. These kinds of clues tell her about the applicant's creative bent and thinking style. If an interviewee passes these initial tests, the CEO has the prospect work with the rest of her staff on a mock design project. These diverse interview tools give her a good indication about the prospect's ability to combine creativity and organizational skills, and they help her understand how well the applicant will fit into the group.

One question for pitchers, of course, might be, "How do I make a positive impression if I don't fit into one of the three creative stereotypes?" If you already have a reputation for delivering on creative promises, you probably don't need to disguise yourself as a showrunner, artist, or neophyte—a résumé full of successes is the best calling card of all. But if you can't rely on your reputation, you should at least make an attempt to match yourself to the type you feel most comfortable with, if only because it's necessary to get a foot in the catcher's door.

Another question might be, "What if I don't *want* the catcher's input into the development of my idea?" This aspect of the pitch is so important that you should make it a priority: Find a part of your proposal that you are willing to yield on and invite the catcher to come up with suggestions. In fact, my observations suggest that you should engage the catcher as soon as possible in the development of the idea. Once the catcher feels like a creative collaborator, the odds of rejection diminish.

Ultimately, the pitch will always remain an imperfect process for communicating creative ideas. But by being aware of stereotyping processes and the value of collaboration, both pitchers and catchers can understand the difference between a pitch and a hit.

Originally published in September 2003. Reprint R0309J

The Five Messages Leaders Must Manage

by John Hamm

IF YOU WANT TO KNOW why so many organizations sink into chaos, look no further than their leaders' mouths. Leadership, at any level, certainly isn't easy—but unclear, vague, roller-coaster pronouncements make many top managers' jobs infinitely more difficult than they need to be. Leaders frequently espouse dozens of cliché-infused declarations such as "Let's focus on the key priorities this quarter," "Customers come first," or "We need a full-court press in engineering this month." Over and over again, they present grand, overarching—yet fuzzy—notions of where they think the company is going. Too often, they assume everyone shares the same definitions of broad terms like vision, loyalty, accountability, customer relationships, teamwork, focus, priority, culture, frugality, decision making, results, and so on, virtually ad infinitum.

Even the most senior managers nod in polite agreement when the CEO uses inflated terms like these, but the executives may feel somewhat discomfited, wondering whether they've truly understood. Rather than asking for clarification—a request they fear would make them look stupid—they pass on vague marching orders to their own troops, all of whom develop their own interpretations of what their bosses mean. In the absence of clear communication that satisfies the urgent desire to know what the boss is really thinking, people imagine all kinds of motives. The result is often sloppy behavior and misalignment that can cost a company dearly. Precious time is wasted, rumors abound, talented people lose their focus, big projects fail.

By contrast, think of the way a high-reliability team—say, an emergency room staff or a SWAT team—works. Every member has a precise understanding of what things mean. Surgeons and nurses speak the same medical language. SWAT teams know exactly what weapons to use, and when and how and under what conditions to use them. In these professions, there is absolutely no room for sloppy communication. If team members don't speak to each other with precision, people die. People don't die in corporations, but without clear definitions and directions from the top, they work ineffectively and at cross-purposes.

For the past five years, I've worked with hundreds of CEOs as a leadership coach, a board member, a venture capital investor, and a strategy consultant. I've also been a president and CEO myself (my company, Whistle Communications, was acquired by IBM in 1999). The companies whose CEOs I've worked with—typically technology firms—range in size from about 100 to several thousand people. In observing CEOs, I've come to the conclusion that the real job of leadership is to inspire the organization to take responsibility for creating a better future. I believe effective communication is a leader's single most critical management tool for making this happen. When leaders take the time to explain what they mean, both explicitly (by carefully defining their visions, intentions, and directions) and implicitly (through their behavior), they assert much-needed influence over the vague but powerful notions that otherwise run away with employees' imaginations. By clarifying amorphous terms and commanding and managing the corporate vocabulary, leaders effectively align precious employee energy and commitment within their organizations.

In researching this topic, I have discovered that many leaders don't take the time to define specifically what they mean when they

Idea in Brief

If you want to know why so many organizations sink into chaos, look no further than their leaders' mouths. Over and over, leaders present grand, overarching—yet fuzzy—notions of where they think the company is going. They assume everyone shares their definitions of "vision," "accountability," and "results." The result is often sloppy behavior and misalignment that can cost a company dearly. Effective communication is a leader's most critical tool for doing the essential job of leadership: inspiring the organization to take responsibility for creating a better future. Five topics wield extraordinary influence within a company: organizational structure and hierarchy, financial results, the leader's sense of his or her job, time management, and corporate culture. Properly defined, disseminated, and controlled, these topics give the leader opportunities for increased accountability and substantially better performance.

For example, one CEO always keeps communications about hierarchy admirably brief and to the point. When he realized he needed to realign internal resources, he told the staff: "I'm changing the structure of resources so that we can execute more effectively." After unveiling a new organization chart, he said, "It's 10:45. You have until noon to be annoyed, should that be your reaction. At noon, pizza will be served. At one o'clock, we go to work in our new positions." The most effective leaders ask themselves, "What needs to happen today to get where we want to go? What vague belief or notion can I clarify or debunk?" A CEO who communicates precisely to 10 direct reports, each of whom communicates with equal precision to 40 other employees, aligns the organization's commitment and energy with a well-understood vision of the firm's real goals and opportunities.

use generalized terms or clichés. They don't want to feel that they are talking down to people by providing what seems like unnecessary detail or context. Leaders simply assume that the exact meaning of their words is obvious; they're surprised to learn not only that their message has been unclear but that their teams crave definitions so they aren't forced to guess what the boss has in mind.

If we accept that the leader's job, at its core, is to inspire and support the organization's collective responsibility to create a better future for the company, then what are the keys to effectiveness?

The Idea in Practice

To inspire your workforce to greatness, Hamm recommends crystal-clear communication about these five topics:

Organizational Hierarchy

When your company reorganizes, quickly frame the change as a way to optimize your company's resources—not to oust or devalue employees.

Example: The CEO of a small software company had to realign internal resources when a close rival began gaining an advantage. He called an all-hands meeting, explaining, "We're in a war for market share. I don't think we're properly configured to win the battle, so I'm restructuring resources so we can execute more effectively. Most of you will continue doing the same jobs, but you may have a different supervisor." He showed them the new organization chart, then asked them to begin working in their new positions after lunch.

Financial Results

Discuss disappointing results not as evidence of punishable failure but as useful diagnostic and learning tools that enable constant improvement.

Example: When a technology firm missed a quarterly goal, the CEO asked his team rigorous questions about what caused the shortfall, rather than placing blame. Instead of worrying about who would take the heat, team members uncovered the problem's root cause and identified ways to prevent a recurrence. From then on, the company's track record for quality was the envy of the industry.

What tools do leaders need at hand for this mission? What mental models must they have? I like to think of good leaders as comparable to skilled locomotive drivers. The train is controlled by a set of switches and levers. When the driver pulls one lever, the train goes forward; when he pulls another, it stops, and so on. When an organization is well aligned, all the managerial levers are easily and neatly moved. They function smoothly so that driver, passengers, and train gracefully move forward as one.

In my experience, five such topics control the train: organizational structure and hierarchy, financial results, the leader's sense of his or her job, time management, and corporate culture. Messages

Your Job

Let followers know that your job is not to provide all the answers but to invite their ideas.

Example: When one CEO met with functional leaders to discuss the company's failure to increase market share, he listened to their viewpoints, posed questions, and challenged opinions rather than stating his own theory. He then assigned a task force to address the problem. The team generated numerous recovery plans, the most compelling of which was implemented. The plan produced the desired market-share gains in the next three quarters.

Time Management

Communicate the importance of using time strategically, rather than trying to get more things done faster. Ask where you can best focus your team's energy. By understanding that you have a choice about how limited time can be used, you can free up needed resources to focus on your most important goals.

Corporate Culture

Create a healthy culture by articulating the right goals and defining criteria for success.

Example: The CEO of a telephony-software company runs his firm like a high-performing sports team. He displays metrics—sales, expenses, revenues—on a scoreboard for all to see. And he clearly defines what success looks like: "P/E ratio of 15, market share of 20%, 30% year-over-year revenue growth." Large goals—"$20 million by the third quarter"—are broken into strategic parts marked on the scoreboard.

on these subjects wield extraordinary influence within the firm. When leaders take it for granted that everyone in the organization shares their assumptions or knows their mental models regarding the five subject areas, they lose their grip on the managerial levers and soon have the proverbial runaway train on their hands. But properly defined, disseminated, and controlled, the five topics afford the leader opportunities for organizational alignment, increased accountability, and substantially better performance.

Before examining each one, I'd like to address a few possible objections head-on. First, why do these five particular topics matter so much—why would defining corporate culture be a higher priority than, say, defining customer relationships? Certainly, other terms carry a premium in some organizations, but I've found that these five are excellent places to start and are highly representative of the kind of difficulties that exist for leaders as they speak to their teams day to day. The topics not only present the sharpest examples of the dangers of imprecise communication, but, when mastered, they also produce the greatest leadership leverage.

I am hardly suggesting that in defining the five concepts precisely, leaders should become dictators or blowhards. On the contrary, I am suggesting that when a leader defines what he or she really means and sets a clear direction according to that definition, relationships and feedback improve, action is more efficient and on-strategy, and improved performance follows.

Message 1: Organizational Structure and Hierarchy

The organizational chart, because it represents individual power or influence, is an emotionally charged framework even during a company's most stable times. But when the corporate structure is changing, the org chart can truly become fearsome, particularly in companies where, because of the political culture, employees worry about risk to their personal status.

If a CEO fails to take definitional control of a reorganization, with its prospect of job losses, boss changes, and new modes of working, the whole company can grind to a halt. Consider what happened when one well-known former CEO allowed the default assumptions surrounding the term "reorganization" to take hold. A few years ago, Carly Fiorina decided that Hewlett-Packard needed a top-to-bottom reshuffling. She had a fixed idea that reorganizations must be managed with extreme care, and she implicitly communicated her belief by the cautious way she floated her ideas with senior managers. She worried that a reshuffling plan would open a Pandora's box of political sensitivities, especially among middle managers. For this reason, everyone assumed that "reorganization" was cause for fear and trembling.

For two months prior to Fiorina's official announcement, work slowed or stopped as employees, not knowing precisely what to expect or fear, shifted their focus to the upcoming changes. Managers, jostling for power and position, got lost in political battles. Motivation plummeted. Contractors were put off, since no one knew who would be managing which divisions after the reorganization. When the new organizational structure was finally communicated, still more time passed unproductively as employees settled into their new positions. A total of 12 weeks—a full quarter—were effectively lost. If you multiply that time by employee salaries, and factor in the inevitable lapses in customer service and product innovation during the period, you can conservatively estimate the damage to the company.

It may be unreasonable to blame Fiorina for failing to realize that she was communicating her trepidation, or to fault her for not divining the consequences of talking about her reorganization ideas months ahead of time. After all, leaders cannot be held to perfection in execution. But they *can* be held to a standard when communicating a vision and its rationale. If Fiorina had laid out the master plan behind the reorganization more clearly, made her decisions more quickly, and communicated more explicitly, the troops at HP would have gained a better understanding of the process, the reasons for the extended time frame, and their future places within the company.

A leader who quickly takes charge of the communication around a reorganization can prevent the discourse from engendering fear. The most productive way for a leader to think about organizational structure is as a flexible map of accountability for action and, thus, results—a guideline whose purpose is to define goals and optimize resources, not to oust or devalue employees. When a reorganization is presented as such, it loses its reputation as a proxy for personal power shifts, whether real or imagined.

The CEO of a 150-employee software company shows how a leader can prevent political fears from taking hold by keeping communications brief and to the point. Rather than viewing the org chart as a source of anxiety, and communicating that attitude to the company, the CEO chose to see it as simply a temporary structure for optimizing resources. When a new strategy or direction was called for, he enlisted people as active agents of change, so they wouldn't be left to wonder whether they were to become victims. For example, the CEO realized at one point that he needed to realign internal resources because a close competitor was gaining an advantage. He called an all-hands meeting for a Monday morning. "Team," he said, "we're in a war for market share. I get paid to win it, and so do you. But right now I don't think we're properly configured to win the particular battle we're fighting, so I'm changing the structure of resources so that we can execute more effectively. Most of you will continue to do the jobs you're doing now, but you may have a different supervisor." After showing everyone the new organization chart, he looked at his watch. "It's 10:45 now," he said. "You have until noon to be annoyed, should that be your reaction. At noon, pizza will be served. At one o'clock, we go to work in our new positions."

The CEO later explained what he did: "We had a competitor who was showing us a better way to win the business. We were both like captains of firefighting teams. We each had seven people and a full set of buckets and hoses. My team had five guys armed with buckets and two with hoses. His team had three guys with buckets and four with hoses. We just weren't organized to compete and win. I wasn't trying to shift power; I was just trying to optimize our resources. I wasn't willing to let this change be viewed as a political event. I wanted it to be seen as a business necessity to remain competitive."

Obviously, it's one thing to shift personnel in a 150-person company and quite another to do so in a giant corporation like HP. But I would argue that the value of clear, honest, explicit communication rises exponentially with the size of the organization. In fact, a large company can be reshuffled much more quickly when the CEO deliberately decides not to inflate the political balloon and won't tolerate others doing so.

Having gathered the data and made her decision, Fiorina was under no obligation to provide previews of coming attractions. Within 48 hours of the announcement, she might have held a companywide meeting, complete with a Webcast, to explain why the change was necessary. To keep people's minds off who was headed down and who was headed up, she could have asked everyone involved in the changes to identify and submit, in short order, explicit goals for the next 60 days. She thus would have communicated that the organization chart has nothing to do with politics and everything to do with organizational effectiveness.

Message 2: Financial Results

"Results" is another powerful concept that, left unmanaged, poses a risk to a company's long-term health. When a top executive tells employees they need to "focus on our promised results," senior managers often interpret that as meaning "Do whatever it takes to meet investors' expectations." By losing sight of the connection between employee behavior and results, and failing to take advantage of learning opportunities, leaders miss out on building long-term value for their firms.

One CEO I knew truly believed that the only purpose of his job was to make aggressive predictions and promises about quarterly results and then achieve the numbers by any means possible. By the ninth week of every quarter, when projections fell short, he put enormous pressure on his sales professionals and finance people. His implicit message was: "These are the results I need; I don't care how you get it done." He fully expected the company to thrive.

Quite the opposite occurred. Because the CEO defined "results" so narrowly and failed to properly motivate or compensate his selling team, the sales force had no compunction about stuffing the sales channel. Though the company never met with any punitive action, its poor practices forced recalculations of results and exposed it to huge write-downs. Revenues stalled at $10 million a quarter, and the company was eventually acquired at a discount to its annual revenues.

In the long term, consistently positive results spring from intelligent strategy and an incessant focus on quality of execution. Think of a golf pro like Tiger Woods, whose best bet for winning major championships is to master his aim, setup, and swing. Once the ball is in the air, there is no way to control it; it will land where it will. Similarly, effective leaders understand that there is more leverage in using quarterly results as a metric for long-term improvement than in worrying only about short-term market wins. By using results as a diagnostic tool in the service of improving future execution, and by asking employees to participate in the analysis, effective leaders encourage honesty and engage their troops in open dialogue. Employees are more likely to generate good ideas, and the firm is more likely to surpass financial expectations quarter after quarter.

I had the pleasure of working for six years under John Adler, former CEO of the technology firm Adaptec. During his 12 years at the helm, Adler drove the company's valuation from $100 million to over $5 billion because he had a very healthy attitude about business goals and financial results. For him, results were not a punitive weapon but a useful diagnostic and learning tool. When the firm, at one point, missed a quarterly goal, he and his management team analyzed all the factors contributing to the shortfall. They discovered that, as a result of an unusual quality-control issue, the company had been unable to make some end-of-quarter shipments. Instead of reacting emotionally and assigning blame, Adler asked rigorous questions of the senior management team, which was able to uncover the root cause of the problem. He communicated this information broadly to ensure organizational learning. By focusing on and taking responsibility for the truth, Adler made others in the company feel safe to discuss the issue without fear of an emotional response that might lead to arbitrary punishment.

Through his actions, Adler sent an implicit message that the past was over and tomorrow was another day. Rather than being immobilized by uncertainty and wondering who would be forced to take the heat, software engineers and quality assurance technicians worked together to improve their processes to minimize the probability of missing sales projections because of last-minute quality or manufacturing glitches. From that point forward, the company's track record for quality was the envy of the industry. By adjusting his "swing," Adler was able to achieve accurate, consistently excellent results for the duration of his tenure.

Message 3: The Leader's Sense of His or Her Job

CEOs wear many hats and play many roles in the service of leadership, but, surrounded by people who seek their feedback and approval, some fall into the trap of thinking that their responsibility is to be the person who has all the answers. (This is especially true of entrepreneurial CEOs who are also founders, because their identities are closely tied with their companies.) The "answer man" falsely believes himself to be the final arbiter of conflicts, decisions, and dilemmas. This puts him in a very lonely, isolated position where information becomes unreliable and useful input is stifled.

A CEO I'll call Jim, who ran a once blazingly successful and now defunct desktop-publishing software firm, had been told his whole life that he was brilliant—and he was. The recipient of an MBA from Stanford and a PhD from MIT and the holder of ten software patents, Jim was also a Midas: Everything he touched seemed to turn to gold. It wasn't much of a leap for him to assume that because he was so smart, he necessarily knew what was best for the company. Jim took great comfort in this assumption; indeed, since he was deeply insecure in other leadership areas, his identity rested on it.

Though Jim made a point of hiring the best and the brightest from top engineering and business schools, he didn't listen to his new team. Strategy, for example, was not Jim's strongest suit, but he believed he knew best how to combat competitive threats. When his managers made suggestions for staving off the competition, Jim ignored them, using his positional power to drown out discussion. He'd say of a rival company: "There's no way those guys could be close to our technology. I've met the CEO there and I know we can beat them. I will explain what we have to do." While forceful and somewhat persuasive, he was out of touch with market reality, and his team knew it. Frustrated, his managers soon grasped the implicit message that they were neither heard nor valued, and they began to flee the company, taking much intellectual capital with them. Jim, oblivious to perceptions of his own behavior, was baffled by the exodus, telling himself that the people who left didn't "get it."

Effective leaders, by contrast, understand that their role is to bring out the answers in others. They do this by very clearly and explicitly seeking contributions, challenges, and collaboration from the people who report to them, using their positional power not to dominate but rather to drive the decision-making process. The more collaborative and apolitical that process is, the less isolated the leader, and the greater the likelihood that the business strategy will be grounded in reality.

Contrast Jim's understanding and communication of his role to that of a CEO I'll call Chris, who ran a technology research firm. Chris, too, was brilliant and confident—top of his class at Harvard and a military hero in the Gulf War—but instead of expressing his intelligence arrogantly, he conveyed curiosity. In functional meetings, he communicated that for the duration of the session, he wouldn't wield his positional power as CEO but instead would be just another contributor of ideas. He listened to everyone's point of view before expressing his own. He posed questions and challenged opinions. In one meeting with his marketing team, he listened to presentations from public relations, marketing, and advertising managers. When he finally spoke, he noted that the company had outspent competitors in a bid to raise visibility for its flagship product but had yet to make a dent in competitors' market share. He asked that a smaller group convene within a week to find out why. Aware that the "boss's answer" would stifle the group's creativity and thus do more harm than good, he resisted the temptation to state his own theory.

In asking his team to be accountable for diagnosing the problem, Chris didn't accuse anyone or cast blame. He thereby conveyed that his role was to help the team process information. He made it clear to the people who worked for him that it was not his job to provide the answers, but rather to help find the best solutions. His authentically collaborative approach encouraged the smart people around him to contribute their ideas. The task force generated a half dozen thoughtful and feasible theories and several comprehensive recovery plans, the most compelling of which was put into action. It produced the hoped-for changes in market share in the next three quarters. In the

Change your mind-set

When executives assume that managerial topics are understood the same way by everyone, they surrender the opportunity to lead effectively. Leaders who explicitly say what they mean are better able to leverage the energy and commitment of their followers.

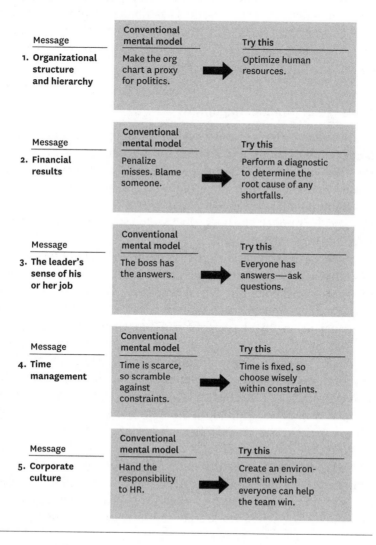

Message	Conventional mental model	Try this
1. Organizational structure and hierarchy	Make the org chart a proxy for politics.	Optimize human resources.
2. Financial results	Penalize misses. Blame someone.	Perform a diagnostic to determine the root cause of any shortfalls.
3. The leader's sense of his or her job	The boss has the answers.	Everyone has answers—ask questions.
4. Time management	Time is scarce, so scramble against constraints.	Time is fixed, so choose wisely within constraints.
5. Corporate culture	Hand the responsibility to HR.	Create an environment in which everyone can help the team win.

process, several ideas for other successful marketing campaigns were born. As a result of his leadership, Chris's firm established itself as a powerhouse of intellectual capital in the technology arena. His company is now regarded as a unique source of market information and is paid handsome fees to publish its findings.

Like the Level 5 leaders Jim Collins describes, Chris led by separating his ego from his job. Leaders like Chris understand that their role is to ask great questions, and they know that answers can be found as long as employees feel safe offering them. Accordingly, the entire team moves the company forward.

Message 4: Time Management

Every executive feels that time is in short supply. Organizers, time management classes, and administrative assistants remind us of the time we don't have. Obsessed with deadlines, managers struggle against constraints by trying to squeeze, manipulate, and control the limited hours in the day. When the CEO gives employees the message that time is the boss, the "to-do list" mentality can easily subsume important goals.

Allow me to illustrate with an extreme-sounding but true example of a CEO with whom I worked. Alan, as I'll call him, was the busy head of a midsize technology firm in Silicon Valley. A former engineer who was ruled by his Day-Timer, to-do list, and BlackBerry, he started every day feeling that he was "behind," long before the opening bell on Wall Street. The time management system was his scripture, efficiency his credo, and prioritizing his Job 1. Alan's fixed idea was that time was the enemy; he communicated this message to his team, telling the members that by managing time better than their counterparts at rival firms, they could drive the company to success. His obsession with time created a palpable anxiety.

When economic conditions in the valley worsened, Alan was forced to impose a moratorium on head-count growth. Then the company received a request for proposal from BellSouth. Alan jumped at the opportunity to make a big software sale and focused his already stretched workforce on the project. Implicitly, time management became the operational currency of the organization. Alan became even more conscious of employees' use of time, so he separated elements of the project into streams, telling his direct reports where and how to use their hours and minutes to produce the RFP. When he was giving feedback to his direct reports, his first question was about how they used the time they devoted to their work. Despite everyone's efforts, however, there weren't enough hours in the day to keep up.

The company submitted the RFP on time, all its i's dotted and t's crossed, then waited with bated breath for what Alan was certain would be a positive response from BellSouth. But the company lost to a firm with inferior technology. The problem had less to do with the content of the proposal than with the way it was delivered. Alan and his team had created a perfect RFP but failed to invest in any relationship building with anyone at BellSouth. The competitor, by contrast, had developed close relationships with the telecommunications firm. Simply put, Alan's people were so obsessed with meeting tasks on deadline that they had lost sight of the project as a whole, and the customer in particular. It was as if the cooks at Alan's firm had made an exquisite, five-course dinner but had forgotten the wine, the tablecloth, and the flowers and had served the food cold. They delivered what Alan said he expected.

A CEO can be more effective if she communicates to the company that the resource of time must not be squeezed for all it is worth but instead must be strategically utilized. It's a subtle but important distinction. A leader who harps on time constraints and breathes down managers' necks, trying to get them to do too much in the allotted period, can make the organization frantic and, ultimately, ineffective. A leader who communicates that when time is tight, it's better to do fewer things—but do them very well—gives managers the confidence to make the best use of this precious resource. That way, everyone involved works within the time parameters to do what needs to be done.

One leader who understands the importance of communicating properly about time is Mark King, the CEO of TaylorMade-adidas Golf. King desperately wanted to launch an industry-changing product to mark the company's 25th anniversary in the spring of 2004. The golf equipment business, like music, cars, and fashion, is trend driven; King knew that if his company could develop a breakthrough product and launch it at a very powerful point in the industry's history, the company would cement its status as golf's leading performance brand.

At first, King envisioned an entire new line of clubs based on the bold idea of movable weight, and he set all his best engineers working on development. They put in long hours, but as the six-month mark neared, he realized that his objective would be impossible to meet by the anniversary date. He could not ask for more time from the team, nor could he change the deadline. So he changed the goal. TaylorMade would develop a single golf club that would showcase the technology of movable weight, and the product would debut at the anniversary event in front of hundreds of reporters and industry influencers.

Instead of struggling against time, King shifted his choices within the time constraint. How, he asked himself, could his teams best use their hours? Instead of playing beat the clock by trying to do everything he wished, where could they best focus their energy? How could time be optimized? By understanding that he had a choice about how the limited time could best be used, he was able to free up needed technical and marketing resources and focus on quality and branding.

The new TaylorMade r7 quad driver, unveiled on the anniversary, garnered rave reviews. PGA and European Tour golfers snapped it up. By the time the 2004 PGA and European tours came to an end, half the professionals worldwide owned the new driver, guaranteeing its popularity among the golfing public. A dozen additional products followed, completing the team's vision for the line of clubs. The meal was well planned, cooked, and served. Today, TaylorMade is the fastest growing golf-equipment firm in the world, and its r7 driver is the flagship product in a multihundred-million-dollar product line.

Alan, the technology company CEO, sent the message that time was to be fought against, and he set unreasonable expectations.

84 Great Things

TO GET AN IDEA OF what can happen when a CEO manages time constraints by setting reasonable expectations, imagine that you have seven direct reports, each of whom commits to completing no more than three important, very doable initiatives each quarter. If these reports and their teams meet their goals, four quarters will yield 84 significant accomplishments. If your company were able to do anywhere near 84 significant things in a single year, the results would no doubt be astonishing. The real enemy to accomplishing 84 great things is the temptation to work on the 85th objective and beyond before, or at the expense of, the higher-priority goals. To keep people on track, a leader must communicate objectives very clearly and demand that action flow to the real priorities first.

Mark King's message was that time was not the enemy, just a fact of the situation, and there were other, more controllable levers that could be used to meet the challenges at hand. Alan saw time as a fearsome, inflexible monster, best overcome by brute force; King saw it as a neutral phenomenon, best handled with flexibility. Both men had a strong vision of what success would look like, but King was willing to make trade-offs in the service of quality. (See the sidebar "84 Great Things.")

Message 5: Corporate Culture

What is corporate culture, and why is communicating clearly and precisely about it important? Culture is not created by declaration; it derives from expectations focused on winning. You can only have a culture that encourages performance if you hire the right people, require them to behave in a way that is consistent with the values the company espouses, and implement processes that will allow the company to win in the marketplace.

CEOs who fail to define success and communicate their vision of it, and fail to make their expectations clear to employees, produce meaningless cultures. The silly cultural activity arising from the high-tech bubble of the late 1990s is a wonderful example. I remember one Silicon Valley CEO who opened the "culture cupboard" and fed employees with all kinds of treats—Friday beer bashes, foosball tables, and the like. He even hired a "chief culture officer," an HR executive whose job was making employees feel fleetingly happy, even when the company lost a client or had a bad quarter. The idea was that if people felt good, if they were "empowered" and were working together, then good results would follow naturally. It was all about employee morale and attitude and teamwork. But managers lost sight of core business metrics. In the end, people wanted to work for a firm that did more than cheerlead them—they wanted a share in a successful IPO. Eventually, the company was acquired for mere asset value because instead of developing a winning strategy, the CEO engaged in indulgent avoidance.

A healthy culture is created and maintained by focusing on the right goals and creating the experience of winning in the marketplace. A telephony-software company CEO I'll call Jeff runs his firm like a high-performing sports team. A big, football-style scoreboard on a conference room wall displays the company metrics—sales, expenses, revenues—for all to see. All personnel in the company, screened for their collaborative as well as their analytical skills, work on six-person teams (according to the U.S. Navy SEALs, six is the ideal number of participants on any high-intensity project). Individuals are only as effective as their teams; everyone in the firm adheres to a strict set of values and basic standards of conduct. Finally, everyone in the company knows what winning looks like: a P/E ratio of 15, a market share of 20%, and 30% year-over-year revenue growth. If the company's goal is to make $20 million by the third quarter, the goal is broken down into strategic parts marked on the scoreboard. The spirit of the company is a function of its collective commitment to success, not the most recent company outing. Successful companies are places where people want to come to work—not to be coddled but to make a difference.

In companies with healthy cultures, employees aren't kept in the dark; rather, they are supported in the belief that they are part of an exciting future. They come to work with a fire inside them, a result of clearly stated leadership and business practices that everyone explicitly understands. Every person in the company knows how to individually contribute to its future.

By recognizing the impact of clear and direct communication and seeking feedback from their teams, leaders leverage, rather than abuse, their positional power. The most effective leaders I know, CEOs who understand that the risks of miscommunication are very high, ask themselves the following questions on their way to work: What needs to happen today so that we can get where we want to go? Where is there confusion in my company? What vague belief or notion can I clarify or debunk today? What have I not communicated completely or clearly? What kinds of things are people taking for granted?

In the end, the power of clear communication is really a game of leverage. A CEO who communicates precisely to ten direct reports, each of whom communicates with equal precision to 40 other talented employees, effectively aligns the organization's commitment and energy around a clear, well-understood, shared vision of the company's real goals, priorities, and opportunities. He or she saves the company time, money, and resources and allows extraordinary things to happen.

Originally published in May 2006. Reprint R0605G

Taking the Stress Out of Stressful Conversations

by Holly Weeks

WE LIVE BY TALKING. That's just the kind of animal we are. We chatter and tattle and gossip and jest. But sometimes—more often than we'd like—we have stressful conversations, those sensitive exchanges that can hurt or haunt us in ways no other kind of talking does. Stressful conversations are unavoidable in life, and in business they can run the gamut from firing a subordinate to, curiously enough, receiving praise. But whatever the context, stressful conversations differ from other conversations because of the emotional loads they carry. These conversations call up embarrassment, confusion, anxiety, anger, pain, or fear—if not in us, then in our counterparts. Indeed, stressful conversations cause such anxiety that most people simply avoid them. This strategy is not necessarily wrong. One of the first rules of engagement, after all, is to pick your battles. Yet sometimes it can be extremely costly to dodge issues, appease difficult people, and smooth over antagonisms because the fact is that avoidance usually makes a problem or relationship worse.

Since stressful conversations are so common—and so painful—why don't we work harder to improve them? The reason is precisely because our feelings are so enmeshed. When we are not emotionally entangled in an issue, we know that conflict is normal, that it can be resolved—or at least managed. But when feelings get stirred up, most of us are thrown off balance. Like a quarterback who chokes in a tight play, we lose all hope of ever making it to the goal line.

For the past 20 years, I have been teaching classes and conducting workshops at some of the top corporations and universities in the United States on how to communicate during stressful conversations. With classrooms as my laboratory, I have learned that most people feel incapable of talking through sensitive issues. It's as though all our skills go out the window and we can't think usefully about what's happening or what we could do to get good results.

Stressful conversations, though, need not be this way. I have seen that managers can improve difficult conversations unilaterally if they approach them with greater self-awareness, rehearse them in advance, and apply just three proven communication techniques. Don't misunderstand me: There will never be a cookie-cutter approach to stressful conversations. There are too many variables and too much tension, and the interactions between people in difficult situations are always unique. Yet nearly every stressful conversation can be seen as an amalgam of a limited number of basic conversations, each with its own distinct set of problems. In the following pages, we'll explore how you can anticipate and handle those problems. But first, let's look at the three basic stressful conversations that we bump up against most often in the workplace.

"I Have Bad News for You"

Delivering unpleasant news is usually difficult for both parties. The speaker is often tense, and the listener is apprehensive about where the conversation is headed. Consider David, the director of a non-profit institution. He was in the uncomfortable position of needing to talk with an ambitious researcher, Jeremy, who had a much higher opinion of his job performance than others in the organization did. The complication for David was that, in the past, Jeremy had received artificially high evaluations. There were several reasons for this. One had to do with the organization's culture: The nonprofit was not a confrontational kind of place. Additionally, Jeremy had tremendous confidence in both his own abilities and the quality of

Idea in Brief

Stressful conversations are unavoidable in life. In business, they can run the gamut from firing a subordinate to, curiously enough, receiving praise. But whatever the context, stressful conversations carry a heavy emotional load. Indeed, stressful conversations cause such anxiety that most people simply avoid them. Yet it can be extremely costly to dodge issues, appease difficult people, and smooth over antagonisms; avoidance usually only worsens a problem or a relationship. Using vivid examples of the three basic stressful conversations that people bump up against most often in the workplace, the author explains how managers can improve those interactions unilaterally. To begin with, they should approach the situations with greater self-awareness. Awareness building is not about endless self-analysis; much of it simply involves making tacit knowledge about oneself more explicit. Knowing how you react in a stressful situation will teach you a lot about your trouble areas and can help you master stressful situations. The author also recommends rehearsing difficult conversations in advance to fine-tune your phrasing and tone. We all know from past experience what kinds of conversations and people we handle badly. The trick is to have prepared conversational tactics to address those situations.

his academic background. Together with his defensive response to even the mildest criticism, this confidence led others—including David—to let slide discussions of weaknesses that were interfering with Jeremy's ability to deliver high-quality work. Jeremy had a cutting sense of humor, for instance, which had offended people inside and outside his unit. No one had ever said anything to him directly, but as time passed, more and more people were reluctant to work with him. Given that Jeremy had received almost no concrete criticism over the years, his biting style was now entrenched and the staff was restive.

In conversations like this, the main challenge is to get off to the right start. If the exchange starts off reasonably well, the rest of it has a good chance of going well. But if the opening goes badly, it threatens to bleed forward into the rest of the conversation. In an effort to be gentle, many people start these conversations on a light note.

The Idea in Practice

Types of Stressful Conversations

At work, stressful conversations take various forms:

- **"I have bad news for you."** For example, you have to criticize an employee's performance.

- **"What's going on here?"** Unexpectedly, a conversation becomes intensely charged.

- **"You are attacking me!"** Someone hits you with profanity, shouting, or other aggressive, accusatory moves.

Preparing for Stressful Conversations

1. Identify your weaknesses to particular people and situations. You'll avoid succumbing to your feelings and ignoring *your* needs during a stressful conversation.

2. Know *how* you react to feeling vulnerable. Do you bare your teeth when facing an overbearing competitor? Shut down when feeling excluded? Knowing your danger zones, you can anticipate your vulnerabilities and improve your responses.

3. With an honest, nonjudgmental friend, rehearse clear, neutral, and temperate responses. Get out everything you're thinking (emotions and all), then refine your phrasing until it expresses your message—in an honest but nonthreatening way. Eliminate emotionally charged behaviors. Write down your phrasing to remember it later.

Managing Stressful Conversations

Preparation isn't enough. *During* a stressful conversation, use these gambits:

And that was just what David did, opening with, "How about those Red Sox?"

Naturally Jeremy got the wrong idea about where David was heading; he remained his usual cocky, superior self. Sensing this, David felt he had to take off the velvet gloves. The conversation quickly became brutally honest, and David did almost all the talking. When the monologue was over, Jeremy stared icily at the floor. He got up in stiff silence and left. David was relieved. From his point of view, the interaction had been painful but swift. There was not too much blood on the floor, he observed wryly. But two days later,

Stressful Conversation	Gambit	Reason for Gambit	Example
"I have bad news for you"	**Honor thy partner:** Start by acknowledging your part in the problem.	You'll help your listener hear your difficult message, without provoking him.	David has to tell Jeremy his cruel humor alienates coworkers. David says, "I share responsibility because I've been reluctant to speak openly with you about these difficulties."
"What's going on here?"	**Disarm thy partner:** Grant your partner his perceptions, and restate your intentions.	You'll change confrontation into agreement without resorting to appeasement. No one loses face.	Elizabeth lists project tasks on a white board and says, "Is that it then?" Rafael snipes, "Who told *you* to assign work to me?" Elizabeth says, "I can see why you took what I said that way. That wasn't what I meant. Let's go over this list again."
"You are attacking me!"	**Fight tactics, not people:** Name the aggressive tactic your partner's using.	You neutralize the tactic without going on the offensive or being intimidated.	When Karen botches a presentation and senses her colleague Nick's disapproval, she lashes out. He says, "I don't know how to talk about what went wrong. Your take on what happened is so different from mine."

Jeremy handed in his resignation, taking a lot of institutional memory—and talent—with him.

"What's Going On Here?"

Often we have stressful conversations thrust upon us. Indeed, some of the worst conversations—especially for people who are conflict averse—are the altogether unexpected ones that break out like crackling summer storms. Suddenly the conversation becomes intensely charged emotionally, and electricity flies in all directions.

What's worse, nothing makes sense. We seem to have been drawn into a black cloud of twisted logic and altered sensibilities.

Consider the case of Elizabeth and Rafael. They were team leaders working together on a project for a major consulting firm. It seemed that everything that could have gone wrong on the project had, and the work was badly bogged down. The two consultants were meeting to revise their schedule, given the delays, and to divide up the discouraging tasks for the week ahead. As they talked, Elizabeth wrote and erased on the white board. When she had finished, she looked at Rafael and said matter-of-factly, "Is that it, then?"

Rafael clenched his teeth in frustration. "If you say so," he sniped.

Elizabeth recoiled. She instantly replayed the exchange in her mind but couldn't figure out what had provoked Rafael. His reaction seemed completely disconnected from her comment. The most common reaction of someone in Elizabeth's place is to guiltily defend herself by denying Rafael's unspoken accusation. But Elizabeth was uneasy with confrontation so she tried appeasement. "Rafael," she stammered, "I'm sorry. Is something wrong?"

"Who put you in charge?" he retorted. "Who told you to assign work to me?"

Clearly, Rafael and Elizabeth have just happened into a difficult conversation. Some transgression has occurred, but Elizabeth doesn't know exactly what it is. She feels blindsided—her attempt to expedite the task at hand has clearly been misconstrued. Rafael feels he's been put in a position of inferiority by what he sees as Elizabeth's controlling behavior. Inexplicably, there seem to be more than two people taking part in this conversation, and the invisible parties are creating lots of static. What childhood experience, we may wonder, is causing Elizabeth to assume that Rafael's tension is automatically her fault? And who is influencing Rafael's perception that Elizabeth is taking over? Could it be his father? His wife? It's impossible to tell. At the same time, it's hard for us to escape the feeling that Rafael is overreacting when he challenges Elizabeth about her alleged need to take control.

Elizabeth felt Rafael's resentment like a wave and she apologized again. "Sorry. How do you want the work divided?" Deferring to

Rafael in this way smoothed the strained atmosphere for the time being. But it set a precedent for unequal status that neither Elizabeth nor the company believed was correct. Worse, though Rafael and Elizabeth remained on the same team after their painful exchange, Elizabeth chafed under the status change and three months later transferred out of the project.

"You Are Attacking Me!"

Now let's turn our attention to aggressively stressful conversations, those in which people use all kinds of psychological and rhetorical mechanisms to throw their counterparts off balance, to undermine their positions, even to expose and belittle them. These "thwarting tactics" take many forms—profanity, manipulation, shouting—and not everyone is triggered or stumped by the same ones. The red zone is not the thwarting tactic alone but the pairing of the thwarting tactic with individual vulnerability.

Consider Nick and Karen, two senior managers working at the same level in an IT firm. Karen was leading a presentation to a client, and the information was weak and disorganized. She and the team had not been able to answer even basic questions. The client had been patient, then quiet, then clearly exasperated. When the presentation really started to fall apart, the client put the team on the spot with questions that made them look increasingly inadequate.

On this particular day, Nick was not part of the presenting team; he was simply observing. He was as surprised as the client at Karen's poor performance. After the client left, he asked Karen what happened. She lashed out at him defensively: "You're not my boss, so don't start patronizing me. You always undercut me no matter what I do." Karen continued to shout at Nick, her antagonism palpable. Each time he spoke, she interrupted him with accusations and threats: "I can't wait to see how you like it when people leave you flailing in the wind." Nick tried to remain reasonable, but Karen didn't wind down. "Karen," he said, "pull yourself together. You are twisting every word I say."

Here, Nick's problem is not that Karen is using a panoply of thwarting tactics, but that all her tactics—accusation, distortion, and digression—are aggressive. This raises the stakes considerably. Most of us are vulnerable to aggressive tactics because we don't know whether, or how far, the aggression will escalate. Nick wanted to avoid Karen's aggression, but his insistence on rationality in the face of emotionalism was not working. His cool approach was trumped by Karen's aggressive one. As a result, Nick found himself trapped in the snare of Karen's choosing. In particular, her threats that she would pay him back with the client rattled him. He couldn't tell whether she was just huffing or meant it. He finally turned to the managing director, who grew frustrated, and later angry, at Nick and Karen for their inability to resolve their problems. In the end, their lack of skill in handling their difficult conversations cost them dearly. Both were passed over for promotion after the company pinned the loss of the client directly on their persistent failure to communicate.

Preparing for a Stressful Conversation

So how can we prepare for these three basic stressful conversations before they occur? A good start is to become aware of your own weaknesses to people and situations. David, Elizabeth, and Nick were unable to control their counterparts, but their stressful conversations would have gone much better if they had been more usefully aware of their vulnerabilities. It is important for those who are vulnerable to hostility, for example, to know how they react to it. Do they withdraw or escalate—do they clam up or retaliate? While one reaction is not better than the other, knowing how you react in a stressful situation will teach you a lot about your vulnerabilities, and it can help you master stressful situations.

Recall Nick's problem. If he had been more self-aware, he would have known that he acts stubbornly rational in the face of aggressive outbursts such as Karen's. Nick's choice of a disengaged demeanor gave Karen control over the conversation, but he didn't have to allow Karen—or anyone else—to exploit his vulnerability. In moments of calm self-scrutiny, when he's not entangled in a live stressful conversation, Nick can take time to reflect on his inability to tolerate irrational aggressive outbursts. This self-awareness would free him to prepare himself—not for Karen's unexpected accusations but for his own predictable vulnerability to any sudden assault like hers.

Though it might sound like it, building awareness is not about endless self-analysis. Much of it simply involves making our tacit knowledge about ourselves more explicit. We all know from past experience, for instance, what kinds of conversations and people we handle badly. When you find yourself in a difficult conversation, ask yourself whether this is one of those situations and whether it involves one of those people. For instance, do you bare your teeth when faced with an overbearing competitor? Do you shut down when you feel excluded? Once you know what your danger zones are, you can anticipate your vulnerability and improve your response.

Explicit self-awareness will often help save you from engaging in a conversation in a way that panders to your feelings rather than one that serves your needs. Think back to David, the boss of the non-profit institution, and Jeremy, his cocky subordinate. Given Jeremy's history, David's conversational game plan—easing in, then when that didn't work, the painful-but-quick bombshell—was doomed. A better approach would have been for David to split the conversation into two parts. In a first meeting, he could have raised the central issues of Jeremy's biting humor and disappointing performance. A second meeting could have been set up for the discussion itself. Handling the situation incrementally would have allowed time for both David and Jeremy to prepare for a two-way conversation instead of one of them delivering a monologue. After all, this wasn't an emergency; David didn't have to exhaust this topic immediately. Indeed, if David had been more self-aware, he might have recognized that the approach he chose was dictated less by Jeremy's character than by his own distaste for conflict.

An excellent way to anticipate specific problems that you may encounter in a stressful conversation is to rehearse with a neutral friend. Pick someone who doesn't have the same communication problems as you. Ideally, the friend should be a good listener, honest but nonjudgmental. Start with content. Just tell your friend what you want to say to your counterpart without worrying about tone or

The DNA of Conversation Management

THE TECHNIQUES I HAVE IDENTIFIED for handling stressful conversations all have tucked within them three deceptively simple ingredients that are needed to make stressful conversations succeed. These are clarity, neutrality, and temperance, and they are the building blocks of all good communication. Mastering them will multiply your chances of responding well to even the most strained conversation. Let's take a look at each of the components in turn.

Clarity means letting words do the work for us. Avoid euphemisms or talking in circles—tell people clearly what you mean: "Emily, from your family's point of view, the Somerset Valley Nursing Home would be the best placement for your father. His benefits don't cover it." Unfortunately, delivering clear content when the news is bad is particularly hard to do. Under strained circumstances, we all tend to shy away from clarity because we equate it with brutality. Instead, we often say things like: "Well, Dan, we're still not sure yet what's going to happen with this job, but in the future we'll keep our eyes open." This is a roundabout—and terribly misleading—way to inform someone that he didn't get the promotion he was seeking. Yet there's nothing inherently brutal about honesty. It is not the content but the delivery of the news that makes it brutal or humane. Ask a surgeon; ask a priest; ask a cop. If a message is given skillfully—even though the news is bad—the content may still be tolerable. When a senior executive, for example, directly tells a subordinate that "the promotion has gone to someone else," the news is likely to be highly unpleasant, and the appropriate reaction is sadness, anger, and anxiety. But if the content is clear, the listener can better begin to

phrasing. Be vicious, be timid, be sarcastically witty, jump around in your argument, but get it out. Now go over it again and think about what you would say if the situation weren't emotionally loaded. Your friend can help you because he or she is not in a flush of emotion over the situation. Write down what you come up with together because if you don't, you'll forget it later.

Now fine-tune the phrasing. When you imagine talking to the counterpart, your phrasing tends to be highly charged—and you can think of only one way to say anything. But when your friend says, "Tell me how you want to say this," an interesting thing happens: your phrasing is often much better, much more temperate, usable. Remember, you can say what you want to say, you just can't say it process the information. Indeed, bringing clarity to the content eases the burden for the counterpart rather than increases it.

Tone is the nonverbal part of delivery in stressful conversations. It is intonation, facial expressions, conscious and unconscious body language. Although it's hard to have a neutral tone when overcome by strong feelings, neutrality is the desired norm in crisis communications, including stressful conversations. Consider the classic neutrality of NASA. Regardless of how dire the message, NASA communicates its content in uninflected tones: "Houston, we have a problem." It takes practice to acquire such neutrality. But a neutral tone is the best place to start when a conversation turns stressful.

Temperate phrasing is the final element in this triumvirate of skills. English is a huge language, and there are lots of different ways to say what you need to say. Some of these phrases are temperate, while others baldly provoke your counterpart to dismiss your words—and your content. In the United States, for example, some of the most intemperate phrasing revolves around threats of litigation: "If you don't get a check to me by April 23, I'll be forced to call my lawyer." Phrases like this turn up the heat in all conversations, particularly in strained ones. But remember, we're not in stressful conversations to score points or to create enemies. The goal is to advance the conversation, to hear and be heard accurately, and to have a functional exchange between two people. So next time you want to snap at someone—"Stop interrupting me!"—try this: "Can you hold on a minute? I want to finish before I lose my train of thought." Temperate phrasing will help you take the strain out of a stressful conversation.

---

like that. Also, work on your body language with your friend. You'll both soon be laughing because of the expressions that sneak out unawares—eyebrows skittering up and down, legs wrapped around each other like licorice twists, nervous snickers that will certainly be misinterpreted. (For more on preparing for stressful conversations, see the sidebar "The DNA of Conversation Management.")

Managing the Conversation

While it is important to build awareness and to practice before a stressful conversation, these steps are not enough. Let's look at what you can do as the conversation unfolds. Consider Elizabeth, the team leader whose colleague claimed she was usurping control. She couldn't think well on her feet in confrontational situations, and she knew it, so she needed a few hip-pocket phrases—phrases she could recall on the spot so that she wouldn't have to be silent or invent something on the spur of the moment. Though such a solution sounds simple, most of us don't have a tool kit of conversational tactics ready at hand. Rectifying this gap is an essential part of learning how to handle stressful conversations better. We need to learn communications skills, in the same way that we learn CPR: well in advance, knowing that when we need to use them, the situation will be critical and tense. Here are three proven conversational gambits. The particular wording may not suit your style, and that's fine. The important thing is to understand how the techniques work, and then choose phrasing that is comfortable for you.

Honor thy partner

When David gave negative feedback to Jeremy, it would have been refreshing if he had begun with an admission of regret and some responsibility for his contribution to their shared problem. "Jeremy," he might have said, "the quality of your work has been undercut—in part by the reluctance of your colleagues to risk the edge of your humor by talking problems through with you. I share responsibility for this because I have been reluctant to speak openly about these difficulties with you, whom I like and respect and with whom I have worked a long time." Acknowledging responsibility as a technique—particularly as an opening—can be effective because it immediately focuses attention, but without provocation, on the difficult things the speaker needs to say and the listener needs to hear.

Is this always a good technique in a difficult conversation? No, because there is never any one good technique. But in this case, it effectively sets the tone for David's discussion with Jeremy. It honors the problems, it honors Jeremy, it honors their relationship, and it honors David's responsibility. Any technique that communicates honor in a stressful conversation—particularly a conversation that will take the counterpart by surprise—is to be highly valued. Indeed, the ability to act with dignity can make or break a stressful conversation. More important, while Jeremy has left the company, he can still do harm by spreading gossip and using his insider's knowledge against the organization. The more intolerable the conversation with David has been, the more Jeremy is likely to make the organization pay.

Disarm by restating your intentions

Part of the difficulty in Rafael and Elizabeth's "What's Going On Here?" conversation is that Rafael's misinterpretation of Elizabeth's words and actions seems to be influenced by instant replays of other stressful conversations that he has had in the past. Elizabeth doesn't want to psychoanalyze Rafael; indeed, exploring Rafael's internal landscape would exacerbate this painful situation. So what can Elizabeth do to defuse the situation unilaterally?

Elizabeth needs a technique that doesn't require her to understand the underlying reasons for Rafael's strong reaction but helps her handle the situation effectively. "I can see how you took what I said the way you did, Rafael. That wasn't what I meant. Let's go over this list again." I call this the clarification technique, and it's a highly disarming one. Using it, Elizabeth can unilaterally change the confrontation into a point of agreement. Instead of arguing with Rafael about his perceptions, she grants him his perceptions—after all, they're his. Instead of arguing about her intentions, she keeps the responsibility for aligning her words with her intentions on her side. And she goes back into the conversation right where they left off. (For a fuller discussion of the disconnect between what we mean and what we say, see the sidebar "The Gap Between Communication and Intent.")

This technique will work for Elizabeth regardless of Rafael's motive. If Rafael innocently misunderstood what she was saying, she isn't fighting him. She accepts his take on what she said and did and corrects it. If his motive is hostile, Elizabeth doesn't concur just to appease him. She accepts and retries. No one loses face. No one scores points off the other. No one gets drawn off on a tangent.

The Gap Between Communication and Intent

ONE OF THE MOST COMMON OCCURRENCES in stressful conversations is that we all start relying far too much on our intentions. As the mercury in the emotional thermometer rises, we presume that other people automatically understand what we mean. We assume, for instance, that people know we mean well. Indeed, research shows that in stressful conversations, most speakers assume that the listener believes that they have good intentions, regardless of what they say. Intentions can never be that powerful in communications—and certainly not in stressful conversations.

To see what I mean, just think of the last time someone told you not to take something the wrong way. This may well have been uttered quite sincerely by the speaker; nevertheless, most people automatically react by stiffening inwardly, anticipating something at least mildly offensive or antagonistic. And that is exactly the reaction that phrase is always going to get. Because the simplest rule about stressful conversations is that people don't register intention despite words; we register intention through words. In stressful

Fight tactics, not people

Rafael may have baffled Elizabeth, but Karen was acting with outright malice toward Nick when she flew off the handle after a disastrous meeting with the client. Nick certainly can't prevent her from using the thwarting tactics with which she has been so successful in the past. But he can separate Karen's character from her behavior. For instance, it's much more useful for him to think of Karen's reactions as thwarting tactics rather than as personal characteristics. If he thinks of Karen as a distorting, hostile, threatening person, where does that lead? What can anyone ever do about another person's character? But if Nick sees Karen's behavior as a series of tactics that she is using with him because they have worked for her in the past, he can think about using countering techniques to neutralize them.

The best way to neutralize a tactic is to name it. It's much harder to use a tactic once it is openly identified. If Nick, for instance, had said, "Karen, we've worked together pretty well for a long time. I don't know how to talk about what went wrong in the meeting conversations in particular, the emphasis is on what is actually said, not on what we intend or feel. This doesn't mean that participants in stressful conversations don't have feelings or intentions that are valid and valuable. They do. But when we talk about people in stressful communication, we're talking about communication between people—and not about intentions.

Of course, in difficult conversations we may all wish that we didn't have to be so explicit. We may want the other person to realize what we mean even if we don't spell it out. But that leads to the wrong division of labor—with the listener interpreting rather than the speaker communicating. In all conversations, but especially in stressful ones, we are all responsible for getting across to one another precisely what we want to say. In the end, it's far more dignified for an executive to come right out and tell an employee: "Corey, I've arranged a desk for you—and six weeks of outplacement service—because you won't be with us after the end of July." Forcing someone to guess your intentions only prolongs the agony of the inevitable.

---

when your take on what happened, and what's going on now, is so different from mine," he would have changed the game completely. He neither would have attacked Karen nor remained the pawn of her tactics. But he would have made Karen's tactics in the conversation the dominant problem.

Openly identifying a tactic, particularly an aggressive one, is disarming for another reason. Often we think of an aggressive counterpart as persistently, even endlessly, contentious, but that isn't true. People have definite levels of aggression that they're comfortable with—and they are reluctant to raise the bar. When Nick doesn't acknowledge Karen's tactics, she can use them unwittingly, or allegedly so. But if Nick speaks of them, it would require more aggression on Karen's part to continue using the same tactics. If she is at or near her aggression threshold, she won't continue because that would make her uncomfortable. Nick may not be able to stop Karen, but she may stop herself.

People think stressful conversations are inevitable. And they are. But that doesn't mean they have to have bad resolutions. Consider a client of mine, Jacqueline, the only woman on the board of an engineering company. She was sensitive to slighting remarks about women in business, and she found one board member deliberately insensitive. He repeatedly ribbed her about being a feminist and, on this occasion, he was telling a sexist joke.

This wasn't the first time that something like this had happened, and Jacqueline felt the usual internal cacophony of reactions. But because she was aware that this was a stressful situation for her, Jacqueline was prepared. First, she let the joke hang in the air for a minute and then went back to the issue they had been discussing. When Richard didn't let it go but escalated with a new poke—"Come on, Jackie, it was a *joke*"—Jacqueline stood her ground. "Richard," she said, "this kind of humor is frivolous to you, but it makes me feel pushed aside." Jacqueline didn't need to say more. If Richard had continued to escalate, he would have lost face. In fact, he backed down: "Well, I wouldn't want my wife to hear about my bad behavior a second time," he snickered. Jacqueline was silent. She had made her point; there was no need to embarrass him.

Stressful conversations are never easy, but we can all fare better if, like Jacqueline, we prepare for them by developing greater awareness of our vulnerabilities and better techniques for handling ourselves. The advice and tools described in this article can be helpful in unilaterally reducing the strain in stressful conversations. All you have to do is try them. If one technique doesn't work, try another. Find phrasing that feels natural. But keep practicing—you'll find what works best for you.

Originally published in July 2001. Reprint R0107H

About the Contributors

GARY A. WILLIAMS is the founder and CEO of wRatings Corporation.

ROBERT B. MILLER has more than 40 years of experience in sales, consulting, and executive management, and is a coauthor of several business books.

ROBERT B. CIALDINI is the president of Influence at Work and a professor emeritus of marketing at Arizona State University.

DEBORAH TANNEN is a professor of linguistics at Georgetown University.

JAY A. CONGER is the Henry R. Kravis Research Chair in Leadership Studies at Claremont McKenna College.

LESLIE PERLOW is the Konosuke Matsushita Professor of Leadership at Harvard Business School.

STEPHANIE WILLIAMS is a principal at North Star Consulting and a former Harvard Business School research associate.

NICK MORGAN is the CEO and founder of Public Words, a communications consulting firm.

STEPHEN DENNING, formerly the program director of knowledge management at the World Bank, works with organizations on leadership, management, innovation, and storytelling.

KIMBERLY D. ELSBACH is a professor of management at the University of California, Davis.

JOHN HAMM is a general partner at VSP Capital in San Francisco.

HOLLY WEEKS teaches and consults on communications issues. She is an adjunct lecturer in public policy and leadership at Harvard's Kennedy School of Government.

Index

Smart advice and inspiration from a source you trust.

Whether you need help tackling today's most urgent work challenge or shaping your organization's strategy for the future, *Harvard Business Review* has got you covered.

HBR Guides Series

HOW-TO ESSENTIALS FROM LEADING EXPERTS

HBR Guide to Better Business Writing
HBR Guide to Finance Basics for Managers
HBR Guide to Getting the Right Work Done
HBR Guide to Managing Up and Across
HBR Guide to Persuasive Presentations
HBR Guide to Project Management

HBR's 10 Must Reads Series

IF YOU READ NOTHING ELSE, READ THESE DEFINITIVE ARTICLES FROM HARVARD BUSINESS REVIEW

HBR's 10 Must Reads on Change Management
HBR's 10 Must Reads on Leadership
HBR's 10 Must Reads on Managing People
HBR's 10 Must Reads on Managing Yourself
HBR's 10 Must Reads on Strategy
HBR's 10 Must Reads: The Essentials

Buy for your team, clients, or event.
Visit our site for quantity discount rates.

hbr.org/books/direct-and-bulk-sales

Harvard Business Review Press